"*Lord of Our Emotion.* emotions, but engages the grace, mercy, and ⸺ where we hear so much about abuse and the tragedy of it. Very few times do we hear about the ability of God to restore and renew. This book will do that and more."

— **Dr. Randy Valimont, Senior Pastor Griffin First Assembly an Encounter Life Church**

"Sharon has written a touching, vulnerable story of her journey from a life of darkness into the light of Jesus Christ. Along with personal details and transparent struggles of utter brokenness, she includes helpful scriptures as well as techniques to help others who have shared similar emotional battles. The reader feels the joy of her redemption and the peace she achieves as she walks with the Lord and learns to integrate His new mercies into her daily life. Her story gives hope to those who share similar pain and who may need a picture of God's grace. Most importantly, Sharon gives God all the glory as she effectively demonstrates His work of refining and restoration, His immeasurable love, and His abundant mercies."

— **Susan L. Mayo, Ph.D. Licensed Psychologist**

"In *Lord of Our Emotions: From Redheaded Stepchild to My Happy Place in God*, Sharon Howard shares the poignant story of her journey from unloved stepchild to much-loved daughter of the King. With her fresh, honest voice, Howard tells how she overcame both personal and family challenges through a growing faith that continues to bear fruit today. Anyone who has ever experienced disappointment and setbacks will be encouraged by this thoroughly uplifting read."

— **Angela McRae, Award-Winning Editor, Author, and Blogger**

ACKNOWLEDGMENTS

Dedicated to Jesus Christ, my savior, for His unending grace and mercy.

Words cannot express my appreciation to **Michael Howard**, my wonderful, supportive husband, who provides me with unconditional love and without whom I could not have completed this project.

Thank you to husband-and-wife authors, Alex and Angela McRae, who gave generously of their time to encourage and teach others how to become authors.

Thank you to LTC R. (Bob) W.P. Patterson, a true American hero and author of over thirty books. He and his wife, Arlene, were instrumental in igniting the desire and belief that I could successfully publish a book.

LORD OF OUR EMOTIONS:
FROM REDHEADED STEPCHILD TO MY HAPPY PLACE IN GOD

My story of overcoming abuse and family mental illness to find peace and happiness through God's grace and mercy—so you can too

Sharon Harrington Howard

Copyright © 2018 by Sharon Harrington Howard
Published in the United States of America
Written by Sharon Harrington Howard

All rights reserved. No part of this publication may be reproduced, stored in a retrieval system, or transmitted by any means – electronic, mechanical, photographic (photocopying), recording or otherwise without prior permission in writing from the author.

Unless otherwise noted, Scripture is taken from the New American Standard Bible Reference Edition Copyright © 1960, 1962, 1963, 1968, 1971, 1972, 1973, 1975, 1977, by THE LOCKMAN FOUNDATION. Used by permission. www.lockman.org

Scripture quotations marked KJV are taken from The Holy Bible Authorized King James Version World Bible Publishers Iowa Falls, Iowa

Cover: https://www.fiverr.com/pro_ebookcovers
Editor: Angela McRae

ISBN-13: 978-1-7327350-0-2 (Paperback edition)
ISBN-13: 978-1-7327350-1-9 (E-book edition)

Table of Contents

Chapter 1 - Redheaded Stepchild 1

Chapter 2 - Roots 6

Chapter 3 - The Stepfather 19

Chapter 4 - School Daze 23

Chapter 5 - Abuse 27

Chapter 6 - Trust No One 41

Chapter 7 - Meeting My Real Father 48

Chapter 8 - The King's Coming 53

Chapter 9 - Husband #1 and Church 59

Chapter 10 - Healing Through Journaling 66

Chapter 11 - God's Grace 79

Chapter 12 - Husband #2: Desire Denied 95

Chapter 13 - Childlessness 101

Chapter 14 - Third Time's the Charm: 'Peace' of Paradise
.... 106

Chapter 16 - Faith 118

Chapter 17 - Conclusion 124

Chapter 1 - Redheaded Stepchild

Mom laughed as she said, "Do you feel like you're treated like a redheaded stepchild?" She found this funny and said it often as I was growing up. I was a little girl with red hair who had a stepfather from the time I was five, so I was actually a "redheaded stepchild." My own biological father wondered if I was his child when he saw me for the first time. After all, Mother, Father, and my older brother all had dark brown hair. I felt unwanted even in my own family. The term "treated like a redheaded stepchild" summed up my pain. But it was no laughing matter because it represented years of suffering.

Let's explore the origin of the phrase "treated like a redheaded stepchild." The term appears in American writing as far back as 1910. A red-haired child born to a family of different coloring immediately raised questions about the morality of its mother, and "stepchild" here may indeed have been a euphemism for "bastard." A true stepchild in a family frequently suffered physical abuse from the children and parent to whom it was unrelated. Some writers have suggested such abuse was specifically the result of anti-Irish feelings in the United States, since it was believed that most Irish men and women had red hair.

Here are other ideas: With red hair being rare, a child born to non-redheaded parents was often assumed to be the child of an affair. Thus, the child was treated badly, usually in the form of beatings. A stepchild might be singled out for abuse. But a redheaded stepchild, who presumably looks like his or her absent birth parent, might be abused even more because he or she is so obviously different from the other children.

See why I didn't find that statement funny? I still can hardly believe Mom laughed while saying it. She didn't seem to care that it hurt my feelings.

I felt like the unwanted freak who didn't even have a right to exist. I also heard Mom jokingly say to others, "People often ask what color the milkman's or postman's hair was, ha-ha." I don't believe Mom was unfaithful because both she and my father are of Irish and English descent, but it certainly hurt to hear these things.

My earthly stepfather might have never adopted me, but I'm now the daughter of the most-high king and have been grafted into the family of the one who matters the most—the family of God!

Rom. 8:14 (King James Version) For as many as are led by the Spirit of God, they are the sons [daughters] of God.

Rom. 8:17a (KJV) And if children, then heirs; heirs of God, and joint-heirs with Christ.

Maybe you've felt unloved or that you don't fit in. This book is the story of how I accepted Jesus as my savior and how God's Holy Spirit allowed me to overcome depression, anxiety, lack of self-confidence, self-loathing, and feeling like a "redheaded stepchild." I was able to find true joy in knowing that I'm the daughter of the King (aka "princess") and now rest in my "happy place in God." Jesus showed me that I am victorious. By God's grace, I have entered the place that the Bible describes as "peace that passes all understanding" in order to reach mental and spiritual *rest*. My prayer is that this book will inspire you to lean on God, seek available resources, and rise above any and all negative circumstances in which you find yourself. With God's help, I've achieved true forgiveness, and I rest in the assurance that God's Holy Spirit resides in me and uses me in ministry. You can experience this forgiveness and assurance too.

I can honestly say now that I forgive all the adults in my life who should have protected me but instead abused or neglected me, whether intentionally or unintentionally.

Rom. 3:23 (KJV) For all have sinned, and come short of the glory of God.

Rom. 8:28 (KJV) And we know that all things work together for good **to them that love God***, to them who are the called according to his purpose.*

Matt. 6:14 (KJV) For if ye forgive men their trespasses, your heavenly Father will also forgive you.

How precious it is that God fills us with His Holy Spirit if we ask. This allows us to endure all things and the ability to *forgive* all things.

Eph. 4:32 (KJV) And be ye kind one to another, tenderhearted, **forgiving one another,** *even as God for Christ's sake hath forgiven you.*

Mark 11:26 (KJV) But if ye do not forgive, neither will your Father which is in heaven forgive your trespasses.

God's grace *is* sufficient, and He who made heaven and earth will strengthen and keep you!

2 Cor. 12:9 (KJV) And he said unto me, My grace is sufficient for thee: for my strength is made perfect in weakness. Most gladly therefore will I rather glory in my infirmities, that the power of Christ may rest upon me.

Ps. 36:7 (KJV) How excellent is thy lovingkindness, O God! Therefore the children of men put their trust under the shadow of thy wings.

You are worth the effort to accomplish emotional freedom. God created us in His image and wants us to overcome obstacles. Stretch yourself to be more than you ever thought possible.

My favorite scripture will always be:

Phil. 4:6-7 (New American Standard Bible) Be anxious for nothing, but in everything by prayer and supplication with thanksgiving let your requests be made known to God. And the peace of God, which surpasses all comprehension, will guard your hearts **and your minds** *in Christ Jesus.*

You'll see as you read on why it is so important for God to guard my *mind*.

As I grew in the knowledge of the Lord, I began to put into practice the following verse:

Phil. 4:8 (KJV) Finally, brethren, whatsoever things are true, whatsoever things are honest, whatsoever things are just, whatsoever things are pure, whatsoever things are lovely, whatsoever things are of good report; if there be any virtue, and if there be any praise, think on these things.

It was a long process to realize positive things even existed, much less "think on them," but truth, honesty, purity, and lovely things exist, and they are available to all.

Chapter 2 - Roots

The Cuban missile crisis reached a climax in October 1962 while Mom was pregnant with me, and the year I was born, 1963, President John F. Kennedy was assassinated. The world mourned his loss during my first year of life, and racial tension in America was at a fever pitch. Turmoil was all around, and even though my parents had been married thirteen years, it was a marriage consumed with drinking and physical abuse.

The day I was brought into the world, my father dropped his wife off at the hospital as she was in labor, then he continued on to his job. He returned to the hospital after the workday was over, since his redheaded daughter had arrived that cold January evening. Mom must have been livid that he didn't stay with her. What a sad and unloving way for a child to enter the world.

My father, mother, brother, and all other living family members had dark brown hair, but I was born with a head full of red hair, and my father asked to whom I belonged. Immediately, I was an outcast. My mother would forever be reminded when she looked at me that my father had doubts about her faithfulness. But like it or not, I was here, red hair and all.

Dad wanted to name me Monet, but Mom insisted that the name be used only as my middle name. I can only guess that Dad had learned about and enjoyed the works of the famous painter Claude Monet when Dad was in France during World War II.

Or perhaps that was the name of a woman he met while there. I guess I'll never know.

Mom experienced trouble breast-feeding my older brother and didn't try with me, so we never seemed to bond. Within six months of my birth, my father lost his job, and Mom returned to full-time work. I was left with my father or a babysitter.

My father grew up in Atlanta's Cabbagetown, a community comprised of mill workers. He entered the Army Air Force during World War II at eighteen and became a <u>tail gunner</u>. He flew bombing missions over Germany with the now highly famous Mighty Eighth Air Force (www.mightyeighth.org).

My father's parents were divorced, and while he was serving in the war, his mother moved in with one of his sisters to help take care of an adopted child, so he had no home to return to. He began to rent a room at a boardinghouse in Atlanta that happened to be owned by my great-aunt Flora. In 1949, he met Mom at that boardinghouse. She was a teen making money by helping her aunt with cleaning.

My father was attending law school, so Mom was allowed to date him. I'm quite sure the possibility of her marrying a lawyer was a big motivator for the family to allow her to date a man eleven years her senior. They married in 1950, when Mom was seventeen and he was twenty-eight. Dad graduated law school, but he never took the bar exam and therefore never practiced law. He was a credit manager at a large oil company, and they lived in an apartment just outside Atlanta's famous Piedmont Park.

Mom went to work right away and eventually ended up in accounts receivables in the newly created Atlanta headquarters of Avon. My parents were living large. Dad played golf, and they attended events at the Atlanta Country Club. Their lifestyle included drinking and partying with friends, neighbors, and family for nine years before the birth of their first child, Michael, in 1959. They purchased an 8mm movie camera and filmed their new son at home and on vacations. They purchased a redbrick house in the suburbs and were the typical 1950s family. From the looks of our home movies, everyone was living a happy, fulfilled life for about four more years until Mom had a second child: the redhead. From the outside, life in that suburban redbrick house seemed glamorous, but behind closed doors, there was violence. Mom called the police on my dad frequently, and he was sent to the hospital in Milledgeville a couple of times.

In the 1960s, police often sent people to Milledgeville State Hospital, later called Central State Hospital, for many reasons, one of which was mental evaluation. The hospital was opened in the 1800s, and at one time, it was the largest mental facility in the world. My dad went there twice when I was a baby.

Thousands of Georgians were shipped to Milledgeville, often with unspecified conditions or with disabilities that didn't warrant a classification of mental illness, perhaps little more of a label than "funny." The hospital outgrew its resources; by the 1950s, the staff-to-patient ratio was a miserable one to one hundred. Doctors wielded the psychiatric tools of the time—lobotomies, insulin shock, and early electroshock therapy—along with far less sophisticated techniques. Children were confined to metal cages; adults were forced to take steam baths, cold showers and confined in straitjackets.

"It has witnessed the heights of man's humanity and the depths of his degradation," Dr. Peter G. Cranford, the chief clinical psychologist at the hospital in 1952, wrote in his book *But for the Grace of God: The Inside Story of the World's Largest Insane Asylum*.[1]

Generations of patients battling mental illness were cared for here, as were those with unusual personalities and quirks, and the occasional young person who rebelled against society and authority. There are anecdotes about teens sent to Central State for such transgressions as smoking pot and interracial dating by well-meaning (or simply fed-up?) relatives. Perhaps they figured their errant loved one would be easier to manage after a long round of heavy medication, shock therapy, or the occasional lobotomy; after all, such procedures were more common before the age of antidepressants.[2]

During one of his stays at this horrendous facility, my dad, the war hero, was diagnosed with paranoid schizophrenia. I know he was treated with electric shock therapy but can only speculate about the other methods. I often wonder if people weren't permanently damaged just from the barbaric treatment. But whatever the reason, when he returned home and stopped taking his medications, he became angry and violent. My brother was old enough to pick up a plastic baseball bat to defend Mom by hitting our dad with it. Schizophrenics can be a real danger to themselves or anyone around them. I can only image what it was like in our house during the first two years of my life.

The final straw for my mom came when my dad threatened to kill her with a butcher knife. In 1965, she finally packed my brother and me into their blue Volkswagen Beetle in the middle of the night, and we escaped to Mom's parents'. My father came to my grandparents' house looking for us, wielding a shotgun. My grandparents (yes, both) gathered their own shotguns, threatening to kill him, so he decided to leave. My father went berserk and destroyed the contents of their home. He burned and cut pictures, broke furniture, and punched holes in walls. I was told that was why there are no baby pictures of me.

One of the reasons I would later question where I came from is that there were no baby pictures. So much chaos was going on back then, I doubt any such photos were taken. My father's sister had him committed to the insane asylum once again, and this time the commitment would be final. He spent the rest of his life hospitalized. He entered a mental hospital at age forty-five and passed away still hospitalized, two weeks before his eightieth birthday.

I come from a long line of women who operated boardinghouses in Atlanta. Boardinghouses were instrumental to society in the 1930s to 1950s. Most single young men worked such long hours in the city factories that they didn't have time to shop for groceries, cook, or clean, so they would stay in the boardinghouses since these houses provided a room, a shared bathroom, and meals served in the dining room. My great-grandparents sold their farm in Forsyth County, Georgia, and purchased a Victorian-style home in Atlanta, near Grant Park, around 1940, and after my great-grandfather passed away, my great-grandmother rented rooms.

One of her daughters, my great-aunt Flora, who was divorced from her abusive, alcoholic husband, also owned a boardinghouse in the Virginia Highlands area of Atlanta. With three sons to raise, she became a "high-class" call girl and actually worked the convention centers in the 1950s and '60s. I didn't know why she was able to travel so much, but I liked the gifts she brought me from all over the world. Many years later, I would learn from my uncle Edward how she was able to travel. The men she "entertained" would take her with them.

Flora made enough money to send her boys to a private school and college. This great-aunt is additional proof that God's grace can reach any and every one. I'm proud to say she accepted

Christ as her savior and served the Lord the last thirty years of her life. I believe her persistent prayers contributed to my accepting Christ. She prayed for me and gave me tape-recorded sermons.

One of my other great-aunts, Willie Mae, had been married to an Atlanta police officer in the 1950s, but sadly, he committed suicide due to a terminal illness. After his death, she also ran a boardinghouse on Penn Avenue, not far from the famous Varsity restaurant. Mom and my brother would live at that boardinghouse after Mom left my father.

Mom was working full-time and my brother was in school, so the two of them moved in together. I, being two years old, however, was left with my grandparents (my mother's parents). Not only did I lose my father, but I also lost my mother and brother. Mom left me with my grandparents during the week and picked me up on the weekends. Most weekends, my brother and I were taken to a sitter who lived down the street. Mom went out drinking, so I was left yet again in another home, feeling abandoned.

When my grandmother, Mom's mother, was a young lady, she lived with her first husband at his parents' home in Cherokee County, Georgia. Mom was born in 1933, but there must have been drinking and violence there too, because when my mother was still a baby, my grandfather pulled a handgun out and shot his wife in the stomach while she was holding their baby—my mom. My grandmother made it to the hospital and eventually recovered. She took her daughter and returned to her parents.

When Mom was five years old, my grandmother remarried, so my mother became a stepchild. When she was ten, a stepbrother arrived. But when her little brother was two years old, he pulled a container of kerosene off the shelf and inhaled it. The kerosene entered his lungs, and the doctors couldn't do anything to help him at the hospital, so my grandmother took her son home to die. With the availability of medication prescribed for her shooting injury and now the death of her little boy, my grandmother abused prescription drugs and alcohol. She eventually had another son, my uncle Edward, but the drug and alcohol abuse continued throughout her life.

What an eerie similarity, though, between the first marriages of my mother and my grandmother. They were both abused and their lives threatened by their husbands. I would also experience domestic violence. This is what the Bible says:

Deut. 5:9b (KJV) ... visiting the iniquity of the fathers upon the children unto the third and fourth generation of them that hate me.

We can break these generational curses. We are all sinners since we originated from Adam but can **all** be free from sin by accepting Jesus Christ as our Lord and savior. The decision to accept Christ as your savior must be done individually and **can break any generational curse**. I'm living proof!

I was less than three years old, living with my grandparents while their nineteen-year-old son, my uncle Edward, was away in Vietnam. Even though he had a difficult upbringing with a drug-addicted mother (my grandmother) and might have wanted to get away from her, he didn't want to go to war. I thank God for all military personnel, but it's a huge sacrifice for the men and women in the service and extremely difficult for the family. I can still feel the deep sadness and fear that gripped my grandparents while their only surviving son was in such danger on the other side of the world.

Every night on the news, we heard reports of men dying in Vietnam and viewed actual wartime film footage. War protests were held in most cities. These reports and protests were constant reminders of the heavy losses and horror of having a loved one in harm's way.

Once, when my uncle Edward came home on leave while I was living with my grandparents, he brought a reel-to-reel tape recorder home so he could record voice messages and mail them to his parents from Vietnam. It was like sending a letter, only he would mail a tape recording of himself. The newly available technology allowed families to actually hear a loved one's voice.

I remember sitting around the kitchen table, listening to my uncle Edward giving his parents an update from the war. When he was home, I remember him showing me a picture of a Vietnamese girl he liked. He survived the war to return home, but he never fully recovered emotionally from the war or from being raised by a mother addicted to drugs and alcohol. Eventually he married and had two sons but died a homeless alcoholic at the age of fifty-nine.

Sadly, my grandmother handled all her emotional pain with drugs, cigarettes, and alcohol and in the midst of it, Mom left *me*.

There were no children in the neighborhood where my grandparents lived, and since my grandmother was drugged most of the time, no one paid attention to me. I remember a lot of frozen potpies, since she didn't really cook anymore, and a lot of time watching TV or listening to the radio. If I wanted to spend time with my grandmother, I would sit and watch TV with her. We watched a lot of soap operas and a scary show called *Dark Shadows*. Great influences for a three-year-old, wouldn't you say? My friends were the cats and dogs.

I didn't really have my own bedroom and didn't want to be left alone at night, so I slept with my grandfather. He and my grandmother slept in separate beds, in the same room, and she was often passed out. Theirs was the only true bedroom in the tiny house, and even though there was another bed, it sat in an area you walked through to get to the bathroom. My grandfather was a tall man, six foot five, with a huge four-poster bed. I climbed one of the corner posts, unless he picked me up to place me on the bed. The only affection I received seemed to be from my grandfather, even if it was at the end of day. I don't remember anything inappropriate taking place, but most often we can't remember anything at that age. Sometimes the human psyche will block those memories, and I certainly displayed symptoms of sexual abuse, but I'm not sure if the symptoms were from abuse at that point or from later abuse. However, I loved my grandfather very much and believed he loved me.

One memory I do have from this time is the only memory I have of my real father. I was approximately three years old, playing in the yard at my grandparents' house, when my father drove up. I can still see his white car stopped at the end of the driveway. His window was down, and as he smiled, he waved for me to come to him. I wanted to run straight to him and jump inside his car. But my grandmother came outside, forced me in the house, and yelled at him to leave. I went inside, and as he drove away, I cried terribly. As a child, I never set eyes on my father again.

After a year of living with my grandparents, I was sent to live with my great-aunt Artie and great-uncle Tyrus. Since they lived on many acres, there were no children close by to play with. My mother and brother had a life together in town, while I was shipped to another relative in Stone Mountain. The abandonment and rejection I felt continued. Aunt Artie and Uncle Tyrus drank heavily on weekends, and he was sexually inappropriate toward women when drinking. He made advances and crude remarks to adult female guests and had Playboy-type magazines in his house. He brought them out when he thought we weren't watching but my brother snuck them out when he was ten or eleven years old. My unhealthy, inappropriate influences continued.

Often when I was a toddler and Mom brought me to where she and my brother lived, we were left with a sitter who was an older lady living down the street. When I was four, I ran away from her house. The sitter, my brother, and two cousins searched for me one night in the dark streets and alleyways in midtown Atlanta while Mom was out. They found me before Mom returned home, but the sitter was in full panic and anger, so she spanked me. Mom wasn't too happy when she found out, either but no one seemed to notice or care why I behaved that way. I was a lonely little girl experiencing excruciating pain, but no one had time to notice. I felt invisible, as if I were a burden, without a family and with nowhere to call home. I was starving for attention, but no one paid attention to the troubled redheaded child.

The only time I remember getting attention was when I was taken out in public. Strangers would stop Mom on the street and tell her how pretty my red hair and blue eyes were, but Mom didn't seem to care. I think it annoyed her more than anything. When I went out in public with my grandfather, he was proud of me. He loved people complimenting his redheaded grandbaby. Funny, the feelings you discern at even an early age. Those compliments from strangers when I was out in public are the only ones I recall receiving as a child.

Mom continued to visit bars on weekends, and finally, Aunt Flora, the same aunt who was a "call girl" and introduced Mom to my biological father, introduced her to my soon-to-be stepfather. Mom dated my stepdad for about a year, and five days before my fifth birthday, in January of 1968, they were married.

The timing of her wedding, just days before my birthday is very telling of our relationship and for reasons unknown, my brother and I did not attend the wedding. I believe it is symbolic of the role we were expected to play—invisible. Children were expected to be seen and not heard in this decade, and sometimes they were not even seen. We were seriously told to be seen and not heard many times over the years.

Chapter 3 – The Stepfather

His name was John. He was thirty-nine years old and a warehouse worker at International Harvester in East Point. He was formerly in the Coast Guard and was militaristic in his discipline. He was a heavy drinker and a member of the local VFW and American Legion. The VFW was where he often went to drink on weekends and where he met Mom.

After they married, he moved in with Mom at the boardinghouse in Atlanta and lived there while they had a house built in Conyers. Her new husband lived with her and my brother, but I was still living elsewhere. At the beginning of 1969, we all moved into the new house.

I finally had a bedroom of my own, but my mother was a stranger, and now I rarely saw the people who'd raised me for the last three years. I had no social skills or ability to interact with other children. I had been left alone during my formative years and was starving for attention and affection. I asked if I could call the new stepfather "Daddy." I can't image why that option wasn't offered to me, but I distinctly remember having to ask and was told it would be okay.

He insisted Mom stay home and not work outside the house. Her instructions were to have dinner ready and on the table when he arrived home from work every evening, and it had better not be junk food. It had to be a meat, two vegetables, and bread. I never had pizza except at school. There weren't many restaurants in our small town, but we didn't go out to eat, anyway.

At first, I tried to spend time with my new stepfather. I tagged along on errands, went fishing, or sat down with him to watch baseball and football on TV. Neither of our parents played children's games or spent time doing kid things. He worked Monday through Friday, read the paper after dinner in the evening, then watched TV before going to bed. He smoked cigarettes constantly, in the house and car, and drank all weekend.

It wasn't long before his true nature came out. He had a horrible temper and seemed angry at everything, from his job, to the traffic, to all of us, to the world in general. He cussed constantly, and every other word was the f-word. He called my mother, my brother, and me terrible names, verbally abusing us and belittling us constantly. We were told we couldn't do anything right. He said we were useless and would never amount to anything. Sometimes he threatened to choke Mom if she didn't shut up, by putting his hand on her throat or face.

I remember one particular beating I got shortly after they were married. My stepfather made me drop my pants while he used his belt on my bare legs and bottom. It must have been severe because Mom yelled at him and told him to never lay a hand on her children again. She said she would always do the spanking and didn't want him to touch us.

Mom had an uncontrollable rage that terrified me when she disciplined me. She picked up anything handy, such as a toy paddle or the brush she used on my long red hair. Inevitably, she would end up shouting and sometimes hitting me with my own hairbrush. I was thankful I wouldn't have to endure my stepfather's physical beating again but wished she would protect us from the verbal and emotional abuse.

I wanted desperately to bond with my mother and get attention from her. I had been away from her for many years, but Mom didn't seem to have the same desire. She was emotionless, sad, and angry, and she had her own daily demons. I would learn later in life she blamed *me* for the end of her marriage to my father, and I felt as if she wished I had never been born. She was always angry, and there was no affection. No hugs, no kisses, and certainly no words of "I love you" came from either of my parents. Their words were harsh and degrading. Not only did our parents verbally abuse my brother and me, but they also were that way to each other. They showed no signs of affection, and they seemed to hate each other. No gifts were given from my stepdad to anyone, not even gifts to Mom. Sometimes at Christmas, he would give her money.

As we know through research, a child cannot fully develop without physical affection or touch, and there was no affection in our home. I can still remember the first time my mother and I hugged, and it wouldn't happen until I was nineteen, after I became a born-again Christian, and I initiated it. I know it sounds impossible, but it's true.

As a girl, I was sometimes glad when I had an ear infection because it was the only time I could lay my head in Mom's lap. Then, the reason was for her to apply medicated drops to my ears. It was the closest I got to her and the only time we touched.

I was never taken to church or taught about God, but I remember the large old family Bible sitting on the coffee table in our fancy living room. The room and the Bible were just for show. The room was used only at Christmas and for special visitors (who were rare), and the Bible wasn't opened except when, out of curiosity, I looked at the slick, glossy pages that contained colorful depictions of the most well-known Bible stories. Some concerned me, like the one of King Solomon ready to cut a child in half to reveal the true mother. I found it hard to understand that kind of love of a mother, so that story fascinated me. But other pages brought great comfort, like the ones with Jesus's image. The love of Jesus emanated from the pages. Even if I didn't understand who He was, He intrigued me, and I wanted to know more. I thank God for always drawing me to Him. He's drawing everyone. Will you respond?

Chapter 4 – School Daze

I was sad and angry to have to go to school because it meant Mom would leave me yet again, and most of the children in Miss Culp's first grade class knew each other. They went to preschool and church together. They also knew a lot more about writing and arithmetic than me. But there I was, left alone, with no idea how to interact with children since I had not been around anyone my own age. I was ill-equipped to handle this new social environment.

Teachers weren't prepared for me either since I misbehaved and was already full of rage from losses and lack of development. I was a fish out of water and struggled immensely to fit in. I never felt as if I belonged, and in 1969, there was no talk about ADHD or other disorders. The teachers were accustomed to good little boys and girls who had been raised in church and had their original parents to teach and discipline them. I had been invisible until now and didn't understand how I was expected to act. But act I did.

I tried to learn how others wanted me to act, and I molded myself to whomever I was trying to impress. I must have tried to make up for all the years I was alone, because I talked a lot. I often got in trouble for talking in class, but nothing could have prepared me for the normal questions kids have about parents. The teachers and kids discovered that my parents had a different last name than me, and they wondered why. Mom had my stepfather's last name, Bennett, and my brother and I still had our father's last name, Harrington. This was unusual and a glaring difference from the rest of the kids. Our family situation was rare in the early seventies. I would tell the kids I had no idea what had happened to my real father, and they couldn't believe it. "He left us" was all Mom would tell me.

I craved the attention of boys immediately. Maybe it was the loss of my father's love, as the psychologists would say. I missed out on affection and never received the emotional support necessary for healthy development. But whatever the reason or disorder, I had real problems and was starving for male attention. That would continue for the majority of my life. The boys seemed to like the prim and proper girls who wore dresses, and that was not me. I hated dresses and refused to wear them and was neither prim nor proper. I was a bit of a tomboy. My favorite boy in class lived two houses up the street, and I wanted him to like me, but he was more interested in the prim and proper girl with the dresses. So one day, angry at that little girl, I pulled up her dress, exposing her panties to the boys and all the other children. Well, that didn't help my position with the kids, and the boy I liked so much actually hit me. I don't think he got in trouble for hitting me, but the teacher slapped me on the hand with a ruler for my outlandish behavior and sent me to sit in the hall. Teachers disciplined children who misbehaved by placing them along with their desks in the hallway. I spent a lot of time in the hall.

I didn't receive help with homework, so I found it difficult to learn. Around second grade, I was required to read out loud, in front of the class. I wasn't a good reader, but I had no choice. I had to do it, and I hated it. One day, the word "Chevrolet" was before me. I pronounced it by sounding the word out. I read "Ch-Chevro…let," just like the word looked. "Let." How was I supposed to know the *T* was silent? The kids laughed at me, and I was crushed. I couldn't do anything right, and no one seemed to like me. I felt like such an outcast. If my own mother didn't like me, how could I make anyone else like me? How could I maneuver and manipulate the others to accept and love me?

I tried to get attention and silently suffered when all attempts failed. On the following page is a drawing I uncovered while writing this book.

Look at this rendering. I didn't remember it and had not seen it since I was a child. I look sad and defeated. It speaks volumes about the despair I was experiencing, but no one bothered to notice!

Chapter 5 - Abuse

On weekends, we were required to pile into the car to go to my great-aunt Artie and great-uncle Tyrus's house, the same ones I'd lived with as a little girl. On Friday evenings, my brother and I went to their back bedroom to watch TV while the adults drank, played poker, or danced in the living room. If we went on Saturdays, my brother and I were instructed to get out of the house and go far away.

We took this trip almost every Friday or Saturday, and there were no young girls for me to play with. The neighbors weren't close by, and the ones who were had three boys. They were much younger than my brother, but he played with them because he had no one else to play with, and he was already showing signs of developmental issues.

Woods surrounded the house, and I followed the boys into the woods to play. They didn't really want a little girl around, but I had no one else. I couldn't understand why I was being rejected, but once again, I felt like an outsider. When the boys ran me off, I would walk back to the house, where my family drank and played poker, and try to hang out with them. I learned to play poker at an early age, but they eventually would tell me to go away because the subject matter and language were not suitable for a child.

Sometimes the adults decided to go to the VFW, and they dragged my brother and me with them. Just inside the front door of the VFW was a darkened glass door that required a plastic membership ID card for entrance. All the activity happened behind the door. I always wondered what was happening behind that darkened door because I could hear only the clinking of glasses, loud voices trying to talk over the music, and a lot of laughing. Later, I learned that the guys were playing pool (and betting), and the women played the slot machines, which were illegal in Georgia. While the adults were behind the dark door, we were left in the rest of the building, in the dance floor, bar, and bandstand area that was used at night. Most times, they had the bartender bring my brother and me a Coca-Cola and a pack of crackers. I actually looked forward to that Coke and crackers. That was the best we came to expect from our weekends.

Occasionally, my brother, Michael, would play the drums that were set up on the stage and get in trouble for it. But we literally had no other available activities. We went outside, behind the VFW building, where there was a lake. We often played around the lake without supervision. Employees or other VFW members came out to check on us occasionally but not my parents. Sometimes we were still there when dinner and dancing opened to the public around 6 p.m. You can image diners' surprise to find children playing in the building or out by the lake, unsupervised. Eventually, we all piled back into the car with the adults trying to decide who was the least drunk to drive. The smell of alcohol and cigarettes permeated the car. It was common to ride around with the windows up while family members smoked in the car. But on these days, it was even more disgusting because the adults' clothes and hair were filled with the smell of being in a smoke-filled bar. I would feel sick to my stomach.

My stepfather's excessive drinking caused him to have seizures. Drinking was the only time he displayed signs of seizures. They would cause him to fall down, unable to speak. It was terrifying, and I thought he was going to die. The adults seemed nervous too the first few times it happened, and once, they called an ambulance. The EMTs could see that everyone was drunk. After the seizures occurred a few times, the adults began to ignore them and even laugh about them. When we returned to our home late Saturday evenings, neighbors were in their homes with the windows open. This was before the average home had air conditioning, and since we lived in a subdivision, the houses were close enough for all to hear Mom and my stepdad getting out of the car, arguing and trying to get the key in the door.

I felt terribly embarrassed. Sometimes my parents got dressed up and went back to the VFW to dance on Saturday evenings. They didn't bother to get a babysitter and made us go to bed. When they returned around 2 a.m., I always woke up because they were so loud.

Sunday mornings were quiet, as our parents usually had headaches. Almost every family in our neighborhood, it seemed, attended church on Sunday morning. My stepdad had a rule that we were not allowed to play outside the house on Sundays until after noon, the time that most church services ended. I don't think it was out of respect for God but more likely because he didn't want people to notice that we were home during church hours. Sometimes, my parents forced my brother and me to sit on the couch and watch church on TV on Sunday mornings, even though they didn't watch.

Once, my stepdad took us to a local high school football game. He commented on the good-looking, scantily clad majorettes, and I knew at that moment what I had to do to get attention—I had to become one of those majorettes.

For those of you who don't know what a majorette is, it's a member of a school dance team who twirls a baton. A baton is a metal stick with rubber tips on the ends. Majorettes performed in parades, competitions, and at football and basketball halftimes. It allowed girls to dance to music while wearing white leather boots and sequined costumes that looked like one-piece bathing suits, which they wore in front of not only the student body but also the entire town. I was hooked at eight years old. Finally, I knew how I could get attention!

I was a girl with a mission and soon started baton lessons at the local dance studio. Subconsciously, I wanted to prove to my stepdad, Mom, and other children that I could be successful, and this is what that looked like to me. There were tryouts every year at school, and I wanted to prove I could become a majorette. It required a lot of practicing alone.

I was good at being alone by now, and the baton gave me something to do on weekends at Aunt Artie and Uncle Tyrus's house. The difficult part for me was when I had to go to class and interact with other girls. I had a terrible time taking criticism and correction, especially in front of others. I already thought I was a complete failure and no one wanted me, so I didn't want to hear what a failure I was when trying to be a majorette, especially since I worked so hard at it.

When you begin learning baton, you inevitably hit yourself with the baton—a lot. You're learning to twirl it around your arm, and until you get it right, you hit and bruise yourself. The teacher could tell how much you practiced by how many bruises were on your arms. The pain of learning this skill was the reason most girls didn't succeed as a majorette. But not me; I didn't mind the pain. I was used to it, both physically and emotionally, and excelled at baton. I got in trouble in baton class, though, just as I did in school. As punishment, the teacher made me practice in the corner during class. I didn't know how to interact with others and felt alone and wretched. I was screaming for attention and was such a troubled child.

One day after class, the subject of our hair came up. I said, "I wash my hair every day except Sunday, which is the day when I don't have anything to do." The teacher, a beautiful young lady whom I admired, said, "That's the most important day of the week. The one when you 'should' have something to do, go to church." I remember feeling ashamed.

My parents wouldn't let me accept birthday party or sleepover invitations because they would feel the need to reciprocate, and that couldn't happen. Other children were not allowed in our house to play, much less to spend the night. No one could know about the arguing, abuse, and misery going on in our home. Mom told us to keep our mouths shut and not say anything at school about what happened in our home and to never tell anyone our "business." I was always afraid I would slip up and say the wrong thing. If you live in an abusive environment, you know about the "don't tell" rule because people in these dysfunctional homes have a deep fear of being discovered. Please contact authorities if you think someone is in an abusive home. I begged my great-aunt to take me out of my home and rescue me, but she didn't.

We literally never took a family vacation. We never went out of town. I never took a car trip or stayed in a hotel. I was fourteen before I set eyes on the ocean. That made it difficult when we were asked to write a paper about "What I did on my summer vacation." I had nothing to write. The only way I was able to go to the beach at fourteen was because a couple I regularly babysat for took me to Florida to watch their children.

My grandfather passed away when I was nine. After his passing, Mom again sent me to stay with my grandmother. Mom wanted me to monitor my grandmother's drug consumption. Mom told me how many pills my grandmother was supposed to take and made me watch and count them to make sure she didn't take too many.

There I was, a nine-year-old, asking my grandmother to show me how many pills she was taking. She yelled at me and got angry when I asked. What a responsibility. When I returned home, to return to school, my grandmother died, alone. I remember my mother crying when she died. This stood out to me because it was one of the only times I saw Mom show an emotion other than anger. It actually scared me. I thought I had failed yet again and allowed my grandmother to die since I wasn't there to help her. I felt as if Mom hated me. I didn't have a clue that I was just a child who should not have had to deal with such serious adult issues.

I began to learn that everyone I loved would leave. I learned early that it was safer and less painful if I didn't let myself care for others. Instead of being taught the golden rule (do unto others as you would have them do unto you), we were taught that people were bad and out to get what you have, so you better do whatever necessary to protect your belongings and yourself from others.

Dinnertime with my stepdad at our house was a nightmare, so I eventually asked Mom if my brother and I could eat dinner earlier, before he came home from work. She usually had dinner ready early, and he didn't seem to want to see us at the table, anyway. I figured we'd eat and disappear. Mom agreed, and for many of the last years I lived at home, I ate dinner early and got out of the house or went to my room before my stepdad got home, while Mom would sit at the table with him and argue.

In sixth grade, I began playing the flute. This was another activity I excelled at since I could practice alone. Sometimes my flute would drown out the sounds of my parents yelling. I didn't realize it at the time, but my performances were the result of a subconscious desire to bring respect to our family and to make Mom happy. Maybe I could gain her approval if I did enough. She seemed so unhappy, and since I thought I was the cause, I wanted to make it up to her.

Unfortunately, my good grades, success in becoming a majorette, and playing the flute didn't get my parents' attention, approval, or love since they were wrapped up in their own addictions. My stepdad never went to any of my performances. If that wasn't bad enough, I was being bullied at school. I felt hopeless. I was in such despair that I tried to kill myself when I was in sixth grade. At the age of eleven, I came home and took a handful of aspirin, hoping to commit suicide. I told Mom, but she was unfazed. She told me to stop letting the kids know they were getting to me.

Of course, Mom didn't get any of her emotional needs met through my stepdad or anyone else. She didn't have friends and didn't participate in our school events. She talked disparagingly about my stepdad to my brother and me. She told us how unhappy she was and how she wanted to leave him. When we asked why she didn't leave, she would say, "If I left him, I'd have to work, and you wouldn't be able to be involved in all the school activities that you enjoy." My fault again. It was because of my brother and me that she stayed in such an unhappy marriage. She would suffer for our sakes. She also used us for emotional support when she should have turned to another adult. Propping her up was exhausting because I tried to make her life better. I worked hard to gain her love and acceptance. As an adult, I discovered a description of what was happening back then and my life choices reflect this type of abuse.

> **Covert incest**, also known as **emotional incest**, is a type of abuse in which a parent looks to their child for the **emotional support** that would be normally provided by another adult. The effects of **covert incest** on children when they become adults are thought to mimic actual **incest**, although to a lesser degree.[3]

Clearly, it is desirable for parents and their children to be close. However, in healthy parent-child relationships, parents prioritize their children's emotional needs as opposed to children taking care of the parent's emotional needs. When children are put in the position of meeting the emotional needs of a parent, it creates an unhealthy dynamic in which children essentially become the parents. The children are emotionally abandoned, in effect robbing them of their childhood.

It is important to note that, in most cases, parents who foster a dynamic of emotional incest do not realize the impact of their behavior and do not intend to hurt their children. But the impact and the hurt are there all the same.[4]

Mom kept the whereabouts of my real father a deep, dark secret. She said he left us and wouldn't tell me any more than that, and she got mad when I pressed her for more information. Other children would ask how it was possible not to know what happened to your own father. I desperately wanted to know what happened to my *real* father and yearned with every ounce of my being to know him.

We weren't allowed to watch home movies that contained images of my real father so I didn't even know what he looked like, but in my imagination, my *real* father would one day walk through the front door and return for me. Many nights, I lay in bed crying and fearing punishment for this dream rather than comfort. I cried often as a child, and Mom would say, "Stop crying, or I'll give you something to cry about." I desperately hoped my father would rescue me. I wish now I had understood prayer. How different things could have been if I had known our loving God and could have turned to Him in those times. In my mind, my *real* father wouldn't talk to me as my stepfather did. My *real* father would love me and wouldn't treat me like a "redheaded stepchild."

Abuse comes in many forms, but often the symptoms are similar and result in self-destructive behavior, one of which is devaluing or blaming yourself. God wants to mend those wounds and help you stop the self-destructiveness. Physical wounds are obvious and can be seen, but emotional wounds, even though they aren't always seen, can have terrible symptoms. Many people suffer in silence with emotional disorders while those around them are oblivious because it's not an outward injury.

This is especially true in the church. Pastors feel as though they have no one to confide in, and Christians feel as if there's sin in their lives if they have problems and things are less than perfect. Emotional wounds can be as devastating and longer lasting than physical wounds. The truth is that everyone suffers and deals with issues at some point in life, so please don't ignore the symptoms of your unhealed emotional or mental wounds and don't let them make you numb or build walls.

Going through the pain is the only way to overcome the scars, but God **will** see you through successfully if you trust Him. I highly recommend the assistance of a Christian counselor. I eventually became victorious with the help of godly counsel. I thank God for the therapists who patiently listened and recommended overcoming strategies!

Here are symptoms which are signals of unresolved wounds that may need healing in your life:

1. You avoid specific places.
2. You avoid specific people and/or others altogether.
3. You engage in addictive behaviors or have an unhealthy attachment (drugs, alcohol, cigarettes, men, women, sex, porn, etc.).
4. You lash out and hurt/wound others.
5. You feel sad or depressed frequently.
6. Your mind is your battlefield, and it torments you.
7. You have a secret you've never told anyone.
8. You often have dangerous and disturbing dreams.
9. You struggle or are embarrassed to verbalize your hurt or past.

If you're experiencing any of these symptoms, you may be suffering from unresolved wounds. Take a moment to journal and list the symptoms specific to you. Prayerfully ask God to reveal what might have caused these wounds. Dialogue with Jesus about your unresolved issues and ask Him to direct you to a professional counselor or support group.

Ask God to hold your hand and guide you through the healing process. Then look up relevant scriptures that tell you how much He loves you and ones that say who you are in Christ. There are many ways you can do this. Since most Bibles contain a concordance in the back, which contains a list of topics in alphabetical order, you can look up a topic and flip to the corresponding scriptures. Also, www.biblegateway.com is a great way to look up scripture on-line by subject, but one of my favorite reference books is a small but powerful one entitled *The Bible Promise Book* by Barbour Publishing. I received this book as a gift many years ago, and it proved to be invaluable in my time of need. The table of contents includes Anger, Belief, Charity, Death, Enemies, Faith, Guidance, Hope, Jealousy, Love, Marriage, Obedience, Peace, Righteousness, Shame, Trust, and Wisdom, along with many other topics. You simply go to the appropriate page by topic, and it contains several associated scriptures! It's always worth the time invested to research the Word of God.

Or simply open your Bible and start reading, and God will reveal His heart to you. But first, ask Jesus, the son of God, into your heart to be your savior if you haven't done so already. Simply ask Him to forgive you of your sins, enter your heart and life, and then start living for Him.

Jesus suffered and was despised and rejected, so He understands. Those He loved and trusted betrayed Him. He knows our sorrow. He's familiar with our pain.

Isa. 53:3-4 (NASB) He was despised and forsaken of men, A man of sorrows and acquainted with grief; And like one from whom men hide their face He was despised, and we did not esteem Him. Surely our griefs He Himself bore, And our sorrows He carried; Yet we ourselves esteemed Him stricken, Smitten of God, and afflicted.... 6b But the LORD has caused the iniquity of us all To fall on Him.

If you're being abused physically or emotionally, talk to a safe person, preferably a professional counselor or the authorities. Ask for help and ask a safe person to pray with you, and **never** stop praying and asking God to heal the wounds.

Chapter 6 – Trust No One

When I was thirteen, I was old enough to insist that Mom tell me the truth about my *real* father. Because I was so little when she left him, I didn't know or remember what happened. What she told me would shock me and change my life forever. She said my father was mentally ill. He was diagnosed with paranoid schizophrenia and was locked away in a mental hospital. She then said words that explained everything I was feeling. Mom's words pierced my soul, and I would remember them for the rest of my life: **"He was fine when he had only one child, but he couldn't handle having two."**

Two children seemed to be the thing that drove him crazy. It was the thing that sent him over the edge. Hmmm, who was that second child? You guessed it. Me, the redhead. There it was, finally. The truth. Now I knew what had happened to my father, and in Mom's mind, I was the reason her husband of fifteen years went crazy. It was me. I was that second child who was too much. My very existence ruined everything.

I ruined the entire happy family just by being born. I was that redheaded stepchild who didn't deserve to be born. This was proof, in her own words, that she blamed me for the destruction of the family. Children often believe it's their fault when their parents get divorced. And whether this belief was right or wrong, reality to me was that it was my fault. I already felt as if Mom detested the sight of me. This redhead was a constant trigger for the paranoia and jealousy my father must have felt.

I soon realized I had been lied to and deceived my entire life, and mental illness was something to be deeply ashamed of because no one could know our secret. Mental illness was rarely discussed in the 1970s. Apparently, it was a direct reflection on my mom, and we weren't allowed to tell a soul.

The shame and disgrace increased and added to my sadness. I wasn't sure if I was more upset to find out about my father or the fact that I had been lied to and kept in the dark for so many years. No one trusted me enough to tell me because they didn't think I could keep quiet. I learned I couldn't trust the people I *should* have been able to trust the most, my own family. The painful reality was excruciating. This made it hard to get close to anyone for fear of them discovering my family shame.

The bullying at school escalated, and in middle school, one of the teachers hung a poster on her classroom door. The poster depicted an orangutan ape, which has red hair. The boys began to say it looked like me because of its red hair, and they started calling me "omangatang," a silly version of the word "orangutan," but there was nothing silly about it to me. The name caught on and spread throughout our small school. Most of the boys were calling me the name while the girls whispered and laughed. It was painful. I felt sure the teacher knew what was happening to me as a result of her poster, but she never removed it, and there was no use asking Mom to get involved. This redheaded stepchild already felt as if no one liked her, and the pain of hearing the kids call me this name made me want to die. That name followed me through the rest of my school days.

I was average height for a girl (even now I'm five foot four), and growing up, I was always at a good weight, even though I believed I was fat. Mom was obsessed about her weight, which made me that way as well. She was often on a diet, and many days I saw her eat cottage cheese on a bed of lettuce for lunch. "It's important for a woman to keep a good figure," she'd tell me. I should always try to look good for a man.

I felt the shame of that when I gained weight later in life, but I obsessed over trying to be thin when I was a young girl. In high school, I became addicted to over-the-counter diet pills. When I was a young lady, the only physical attribute that stood out on me, other than my red hair, was my pale, white, ghostlike skin. This was another area of my appearance in which I struggled. No one should be made to feel inadequate due to the color of their skin or hair, but unfortunately, it happens to people of all skin colors. I tried hard to get a tan like the other girls. I obviously didn't get to the beach like most of them since we didn't go on family vacations and we didn't have a pool, so I reclined in a lawn chair in our backyard while wearing a bathing suit, enduring the hot Georgia sun with baby oil or suntan lotion on my body. My brother, on the other hand, got a nice dark tan when he was out in the sun, but all I got was a sunburn. Now, not only was my hair bright red, but so was my skin, and it was painful. And anything that makes you appear different from others can make you feel abnormal. Between the bullying, my feelings of inadequacy, and lack of affection, it's no wonder I started numbing the pain with drugs and alcohol early in life. It's only by the grace of God I didn't kill myself.

I started babysitting my younger cousins at my uncle Edward's house. One evening when the children were in bed, I caught my brother smoking marijuana in the living room with my aunt and uncle. They let me join them, so at thirteen years old, I began smoking pot and drinking alcohol. I started spending weekends and summers at their house. However, Uncle Edward's married friends started making sexual advances to me. He had at least five friends or co-workers in their late twenties and early thirties who were doing everything to me except the actual act of sexual intercourse. This behavior went on when I was between the ages of thirteen and sixteen. These "friends" took advantage of me while I was either intoxicated or high on marijuana.

When I was fifteen, I thought I was in love with one of them and carried on a so-called relationship. We spent hours on the phone in the afternoons after school, and he would pick me up at the ball fields located behind my parents' house. I walked up to the ball fields after dinner, met him, and sat in his truck, smoking pot and making out. I was fourteen and fifteen, and he was twenty-seven and married with two children. Eventually, he took me to his cousin's apartment, where he attempted to rape me, but I fought him off. Following the seriousness of that attempted rape and after meeting a young man my own age, I was able to get out of that "relationship." But even the father of the family I babysat for, the one that took me to the beach at age fourteen, made sexual advances toward me.

Mom had a rule that I couldn't date until I was sixteen. Strangely, she didn't know I was already well experienced with men by then. How she didn't know what was happening to me is beyond my comprehension. It's just another example of how little interest she took in me and how emotionally separated we were from one another.

So just before my seventeenth birthday, I began dating a young man who was twenty-one. We drank and smoked marijuana, and he introduced me to cocaine while I was in high school. This started my experience with more serious drugs and an even more rebellious lifestyle. Somehow, I was able to live a double life. I would go to school during the week, obtain passing grades, perform as a majorette at football and basketball games, and play the flute in the concert band, all while smoking cigarettes, drinking alcohol, and doing drugs on the weekends. Even my closest friends didn't know about my wild side during my early years in high school. I was a chameleon and conformed to my surroundings. After all, I had learned firsthand how to keep secrets, hide the truth, and keep up a facade. I learned that if everything *looked* okay on the outside, then it must be okay.

I became hard-hearted and full of anger, and didn't trust anyone. I spent all my spare time with my new boyfriend. When I was only seventeen, Mom actually let me leave home for a date on Friday nights with a packed suitcase. We told her my date would drop me off at my uncle Edward's house after our date. Of course, we'd usually get a hotel room, and he'd drop me off at my uncle's the next day. Mom didn't care where I was as long I was out of her hair. She usually had her hands full with the trouble my brother was creating. He was in and out of jail by this time. At home, my stepdad and I had a pact to not speak to one another. So, for the last few years I lived at home, my stepdad and I didn't speak one word to each other. My aunt—yes, the one I smoked pot with—took me to a gynecologist to obtain birth control pills when I was seventeen.

By now, the use of speed, alcohol, and cocaine was my escape from pain and reality. Just following our family tradition, as a famous country song states. I learned to separate myself from reality. I stayed active, medicated, and built walls around myself—layers and layers of emotional protection.

During my senior year of high school, I attended school half a day and worked half a day. All other seniors seemed to be researching colleges, but since I was told we didn't have enough money to pay for college, nor did I think I was smart enough to get into college, I didn't believe it was an option. I certainly didn't have anyone helping me figure it out. I wasn't encouraged or expected to succeed. I was told to marry a man who had money.

However, I had a goal. I had one goal during high school, and it was to graduate and get the heck out of my parents' house. I graduated from high school, and my boyfriend asked me to marry him. I accepted, but I couldn't see myself in a marriage if it would be like that of my parents. In a fit of rage, I threw the engagement ring out my fiancé's car window, and we were finished. God protected me, though, because my fiancé was a drug dealer. Once, while we were dating, he thought he'd sold drugs to an undercover officer and feared going to jail but he never got arrested. I spoke to him once, fifteen years later, and he was doing the same thing—selling drugs to the same people. God's protection can be seen in so many ways if we only look for them. Thank you, Jesus, for protection.

Chapter 7 - Meeting My Real Father

Immediately after high school graduation, I took a job at the local bank as a teller and moved into an apartment with a friend. The roommate situation didn't work out, so I moved to a one-bedroom apartment, where I lived alone. Mom helped a little financially to make sure I was able to get established, because the last thing she wanted was for me to move back home.

I didn't grow up knowing my real father's family, and Mom never spoke of them, so I didn't know if he had one or ten brothers. But one of my father's brothers called Mom and asked if he could take me to meet my father. I thank God for His kindness, which allowed me to *finally* meet my father.

I still get a woozy feeling in my stomach just thinking about seeing my father again for the first time since I was two years old. I was now nineteen as I entered the car of a man I had never met before, a man who said he was my uncle, and we drove three hours to a mental hospital in another state, Alabama, to meet a man I didn't know—my father. I was terrified since I was already frightened and distrustful of men but wanted more than anything to see my father.

A girl's desire to know her paternal father is insatiable. I was full of emotions that day, happy to have the chance to see him but terrified, as well. We walked from the car and entered the front doors of the hospital. Immediately, I felt a chill. The air conditioner made it icy cold inside. My uncle asked me to stay in the waiting area while he went to my father's room. I'm sure he had to prepare my father, as much as possible, for what was about to happen. He was going to bring my father out of his room, down the hall, and into the hospital waiting area, where he would see his redheaded little girl…all grown-up.

The two men appeared, and a stranger walked up to me, said hello, and hugged me. I couldn't believe it; my *real* father was actually hugging me. The embrace was awkward and emotionally overwhelming. I dreamed of seeing my real father, but never once did I dream it would be under these circumstances. He seemed to want to know all about me, though. What a strange feeling it was to have someone interested in me. I was stunned and not sure what to say. I told him where I had gone to school and where I was working and living. I certainly didn't want him to know how miserable home life was growing up. I didn't want to make him feel guilty.

While I didn't see anything "crazy" about him that day, I was surprised at how skinny he was. He was not much taller than me, thin and looking a little undernourished. We went to his hospital room, and the attendants brought his lunch, though I noticed he didn't drink his iced tea. So, I asked him if he liked iced tea, and he told me he didn't. That stood out to me because I don't like iced tea either. This is extremely unusual for anyone raised in the south and if you're from the south, you know exactly what I mean. Then I started to notice other similarities which was both refreshing, to feel a sense of connection and scary at the same time. Who wants to be similar to a mentally ill person? This would be the first of many times I visited my father over the years. He remained hospitalized for the remainder of his life, from age forty-five to seventy-nine. Sometimes my father seemed to understand what I was telling him during our visits, and other times he did not. It became obvious that he wasn't operating in reality. His brother had once tried to bring my father to his home for Christmas. But due to my father's cigarette smoking, he almost set the house on fire. So, his brother and his family never again tried to remove Father from the facility.

Our visits were terribly difficult and emotional for me. It's hard to see anyone in this condition, much less your own father. One time I tried to visit him when he was at the Veteran's Administration hospital in Atlanta, but when I arrived, a hospital administrator told me that he had been moved to a facility in Augusta because he was found in a female patient's bed.

Another time, my counselor agreed to go with me to visit my father, as support and probably out of curiosity. When I visited, my father often told me he was sorry for not being there for me when I was growing up, and he was sincerely saddened by how much drinking he and my mother did when we were little. He asked if I drank and told me not to drink. He said nothing good comes from it.

I often fought back tears during our visits. Another time, Mom joined me to keep me company on the three-hour drive to Augusta. We both wondered if she might visit with him. At that time, it had been twenty-five years since she had last seen him. I entered the hospital alone while Mom waited in the car. As he spoke, I could tell it would not be a good idea for her to come inside. He would think about Mom or someone in the family and get angry. He was irate at his sister for committing him to the hospital and enraged at Mom for leaving with his children. Mom would never again see him alive. His funeral was prepaid, and with no other family to make arrangements, I handled the details to make sure he had a respectful funeral.

It was apparent that my father was too disturbed to understand time and distance, and in his mind, he still lived in the 1950s and 1960s. He replayed their marriage and struggles over and over. He spoke derogatory things about our family members, especially my great-uncle Tyrus. The great-uncle I had lived with as a baby had many flaws, but when my parents were still married, he loaned my father money. The money was used to reimburse what my father had embezzled from the company he worked for. As far as we know, my father was able to return the money before anyone discovered it missing, and he never went to jail. Seems my father should have been grateful, not angry, but he wasn't in his right mind.

During one of my visits, he told me that while he and Mom were married and he was in Central State Hospital in Milledgeville, my grandmother, my mom's mother, was there too. So my grandmother and my father were both patients at the state mental hospital at the same time. That was prior to my living with my grandmother. The mental problems in my family seemed endless.

Eventually, I earnestly prayed to God that He would heal my mind and save me from mental illness. In order to fight the fear of losing my mind and the need to self-medicate, I recited what became my favorite scripture, every day.

Phil. 4:6-7 (NASB) Be anxious for nothing, but in everything by prayer and supplication with thanksgiving let your requests be made known to God. And the peace of God, which surpasses all comprehension, will guard your hearts **and your minds** *in Christ Jesus.*

Here's another one I kept handy and spoke out loud:

1 Timothy 1:7 (KJV) For God hath not given us the spirit of fear; but of power and of love and of a sound mind.

Chapter 8 - The King's Coming

Uncle Tyrus had passed away by the time Aunt Artie, whom I lived with as a child, contracted emphysema and cancer. She was never a spiritual woman, so what she told me one evening as I sat at her bedside made a huge impact on me.

She had been in the hospital, and doctors didn't think she would live through the night. She told me that during that night, she started to hear voices whispering, "He's coming. He's coming. The King is coming." She said she saw angels encompassing the room. They were the ones saying, "He's coming." She knew they meant Jesus was coming, and when she looked up, she saw Jesus standing by her bed. He gently put His arms under her and lifted her body off the bed. She felt His love and healing touch. He simply laid her back on the bed and told her it was not her time.

The next day, she was awake and feeling well enough to go home. Interesting how I can remember this as if it were yesterday even though it was thirty-eight years ago. I began to think Jesus might be real. I realized later that God had allowed my great-aunt Artie to live to share this story. She was raised up to testify to me (and other family and friends) that **He really exists** and loves us very much! I'm thankful that I'll see her in heaven one day because she accepted Christ as her savior, and I'll always be grateful she testified to me of His goodness!

Shortly after this discussion, I was invited to a water baptism ceremony, and something stirred inside of me. I decided to return to church the next Sunday morning. It didn't take long for me to understand that I needed Jesus. I wanted the preacher to stop talking because I didn't want to wait another minute to go down to the altar and ask Jesus into my heart, which I did. I learned what this scripture meant:

John 3:16 (KJV) For God so loved the world, that he gave his only begotten Son, that whosoever believeth in him should not perish, but have everlasting life.

It just so happened that the next water baptism for that church was on Halloween night, a Sunday in 1982. I didn't immediately realize the significance of the fact that I got baptized exactly one year after I rented and wore a skimpy devil costume (red with horns and a tail) to the local bar. God knows how to *really* turn things around. Thank you, Lord!

At this point, though, I knew very little scripture and had never really heard of John 3:16. I remembered that when I was in high school, the majorettes huddled before most games to say the Lord's Prayer. The first time it happened, I had no idea what they were saying or where it came from. Mom told me it was the Lord's Prayer and showed me where to find it in the Bible (Matt. 6:9-13). I learned it so I could say it along with the other girls. That was the extent of my scripture knowledge. I attended that little Baptist church for a few months and then decided to invite some of the youth to my apartment for a party. I, of course, was the only one my age, nineteen, who had her own apartment. I decided to have alcohol, and many of them partook. I returned to the church once or twice and knew everyone was talking about me. I understand completely now, but it would have been nice if someone had reached out to help me, because I had a real drinking problem. I felt as if I failed again and stopped attending church.

I returned to the only thing I knew—cocaine, alcohol, and men. I had a huge cocaine and sexual addiction. I thought I would get love from men in this way, and I even contemplated selling cocaine. I didn't care whether or not I died.

When I was twenty, I lost my job at the bank because I wanted to go to a Georgia Tech homecoming game, and they wouldn't let me off work. Because I was living alone in an apartment and desperate to pay rent, I answered a classified ad and took a job selling encyclopedias door-to-door.

Encyclopedias are a set of reference books people could purchase for their homes. They were expensive and the "Google" of that time. They allowed students to do homework without having to go to the library. I would sell in the evenings, sleep most of the day, and stay up on drugs all night. I sold an unheard-of three sets on my first night. I made enough money to pay rent and have extra. However, my great-aunt Artie—the one I lived with as a little girl and who testified to me about

Jesus—passed away and left her sizable estate to Mom. I thought I would inherit the house and two acres, but to my surprise, Mom inherited everything. Even though Mom owned it, I moved into my great-aunt Artie's old house. I turned twenty-one and quit the encyclopedia sales job. I realized I could sit in that old house for the rest of my life and never pay rent. I could stay there and take care of the yard and house, and it would be available if Mom ever needed to sell it. In my mind, I could work just enough to purchase drugs and alcohol and have friends over for parties and continue in a self-destructive spiral, which is exactly what I did for a while. However, that lifestyle required Mom's full control. She would tell me what I should and shouldn't do and drop by anytime, unannounced.

I wanted to go back to work in the banking industry since that's the experience I had but assumed I couldn't because I had been fired. Employers really called and checked references at that time. I decided to call my previous head teller. She was a wonderful, Christlike lady who showed Jesus to everyone she met. She agreed to give me a good reference, so I prayed to God and asked that He help me get a job as a teller with First National Bank of Atlanta (now Wells Fargo). Not long afterward, I landed that job and knew it was a direct answer to prayer. I was learning for the first time that God answers prayers.

Thanks to an employee tuition reimbursement program, I began attending Dekalb Community College at night after work.

I took core classes, like Math and English, but I also took a couple of psychology classes. Now a whole new set of fears penetrated my soul that I had not thought of before. These fears were much more serious than the shame of someone discovering the family secret. I learned about the hereditary aspect of mental illness. I realized I was at great risk of inheriting my father's mental illness. It was now apparent why my brother always seemed so different. He inherited the mental illness gene and had been suffering with it his entire life. I feared it was only a matter of time before the illness caught up with me.

My brother left town, and no one knew where he was for about a year. He and I had no relationship, and he even seemed to hate me. We knew nothing of healthy sibling love. Eventually, someone with a Salvation Army shelter in Florida called saying my brother had been robbed and beaten and was staying there. They sent him home on a bus, and Mom never let him out of her control again. He eventually received disability benefits and food stamps, and today, Mom attends to all his needs and wants.

I lived in constant terror of completely losing my mind and was sure I would eventually need to be locked away. Anytime I felt stressed or had difficulties dealing with life, I wondered if that would be the end of my sanity. Would this be the thing to send me completely over the edge?

I was living at the house owned by Mom and falling deeper and deeper into addiction and depression. I began to have suicidal thoughts. I wanted to die and sat alone on the floor, and I was beginning to believe the house was haunted. I was afraid my great-uncle Tyrus's ghost was there, but I now believe it was a demonic spirit. I contemplated how I should take my life. How could I do it with the least amount of pain? I owned a 22-caliber pistol for protection, and there was a shotgun in the house, but I wanted to take a pill that would be quick and painless. As I calculated my options for committing suicide, I remembered that I had encountered Christ before, and I could vaguely hear Him saying He loved me, even though I tried hard to drown Him out.

I suddenly recalled the sermon tapes given to me by my great-aunt Flora several years prior and wasn't sure if I had thrown them away. I started looking for them since they were sermons of Dr. Paul Walker, senior pastor of Mount Paran Church of God, a large church in Atlanta. Praise God, I found the tapes. They were still in my dresser drawer! I started listening to them, and Christ began to minister to me as I listened to the word being preached.

I prayed, "Lord, I can't do this alone. Please send me someone with 'skin on' to help me walk out this life with you." I wanted to attend Mount Paran Church, but I didn't want to go alone, so God would answer that prayer too.

Chapter 9 – Husband #1 and Church

Suddenly a tall, handsome man came to the bank where I worked and asked me out. We started dating and, unfortunately, sleeping together, but strangely enough, when I mentioned Mount Paran Church, he said, "I've been wanting to go to that church." God was leading me to church any way possible and in spite of my ignorance. I know now this was no coincidence because God loves me and was calling me, but He wasn't calling me to marriage at that time. Nonetheless, after we started attending church and only six months after meeting, we decided to get married. I highly recommend not marrying so soon after meeting someone. Take time to get to know them and wait on the Lord!

It was a small, traditional wedding, and my relationship with my stepfather was so estranged that he wouldn't even attend, much less walk me down the aisle. I certainly couldn't have my real father there, so I walked alone.

Once my new husband and I began attending church, I rededicated my life to Jesus. While sitting in the church sanctuary during worship service, I asked God to remove all my addictions, and I felt something like warm honey pour over my body, which I now know to be the Holy Spirit, and… I was completely delivered! I never had problems with drugs and alcohol again.

My husband played on a softball team at the church, so we met the church recreation director. I asked him if he needed a secretary, because I thought it would be nice to work at the church. I wanted to serve God. The rec director didn't have a job opening, but less than a year later, he was promoted to associate pastor and needed to hire a secretary. He remembered my inquiry and asked if I'd like to have the job. God is amazing! My husband didn't want me to take the job, but I knew I was supposed to be there. Not to mention, the church was so large that the salary was higher than what I was making at the bank. I started working at the church, and for the first time, I was using a desktop computer. After all, it was 1988, and computers were just reaching offices.

When I look back at that job opportunity and how much it blessed me, I can hardly believe it. I obtained new work experience, but mostly God wanted me to get spiritual and psychological help. The church had a large counseling center with licensed counselors and support groups, all within the same building where I was working. I began to see one of the counselors and attend support groups including those for Adult Children of Alcoholics and others.

The resources God provided me were enumerable, and I didn't realize it at the time, but the love and goodness of God was pulling me out of my years of darkness. I was learning how to have a close, personal relationship with God and others. Another thing that job did for me was introduce me to my future husband. I just wouldn't know it for another twenty years!

A young lady involved in church recreation, for which I was the secretary, introduced me to her boyfriend. His name was Michael Howard. Keep this in mind for later.

While still married to my first husband, I attended a spiritual retreat called "Tres Dias." God ministered to me mightily and began to show me my worth in Him. I had a new desire to improve myself spiritually, mentally, and emotionally. I felt as if there was hope for change.

As I began to go after God, though, my husband got further away from God and me. I wanted to start a family, but unfortunately, our marriage was full of anger, just like my parents'. I knew nothing about love and how to relate to someone in a positive way, nor did he. My husband was eleven years older than me, and I was his fourth wife. I couldn't see the warning signs. Soon after we married, he began to physically abuse me. I even went to Mom with photos of bruises throughout my body where my husband had hurt me. She said, "I'll tell you like my mom told me. You made your bed, and now you gotta lie in it. Go home to your husband." So, I did.

I thought my husband was having an affair, and still I struggled with the decision to divorce. I'd been married less than two years and wondered whether I'd lose my job at the church and be ostracized. I felt the employees would shun me and label me a sinner if I divorced, but I found out they were supportive. The pastor I worked for knew I was struggling and suggested I go home and not come back until God gave me a clear answer. I went home, got prostrate, and cried out to God. I finally felt a release and filed for divorce. My husband moved out of the house (we were still living in Mom's house), and he moved in with "the other woman." He ended up marrying her and having a child with her. I was devastated that he had a new baby since he'd told me he didn't want another one. He had a teenager who lived with his first wife. I realized it wasn't that he didn't want another child...he just didn't want one *with me*. Now I see it as God's divine protection again, since a child would have tied us together for the rest of our lives. As it was, I could leave that failed marriage behind. However, it certainly didn't help my self-esteem.

Working at the church was the absolute best place I could have been during my divorce, though. I was saddened and ashamed by the failed marriage, but around the same time, a staff prayer time was implemented. The staff was required to report to the sanctuary first thing in the morning. That turned out to be a huge blessing, as I found myself on my knees at the altar or with my head buried in the pew most mornings, calling out to God. God promises to give us joy for our sorrows, and it was a precious time with God.

Dr. Mark Rutland was associate pastor at Mount Paran Church at that time, and I worked right outside his office. I attended almost all of his services and soaked up every word he presented. His past included attempted suicide and then God's baptism in the Holy Spirit, which turned his life around. Dr. Paul Walker was the senior pastor of the ten-thousand-member church and was on TV weekly. He was one of the best preachers of that time, so I was being taught about God in many ways. I attended a year-long class at church called Bethel Series which is an intense study of the Old and New Testaments. I was also able to watch God work "firsthand". I saw people saved, healed, and delivered. I can hardly believe how blessed I was to be able to learn what I did as a young Christian. I learned a lot about the works of the Holy Spirit and angels, and I learned how important it is to seek God with your whole heart. I finally surrendered to God and gave up my will for His will. I couldn't understand why He wanted my life, but He did. He has that same desire for you.

Below is a list of statements I received when I attended a support group, and they helped me in the healing process. Maybe you can use these reminders too.

- I am capable of making changes in my life.
- I can change the situation, or I can make changes in my own beliefs, thoughts, or behavior.
- As I look back over my life and see the mistakes and bad choices that I have made, I may wonder whether I will ever be able to change this pattern of failure to one of success.

- I know that unlike any other creature in the world, I have received God's gift of free will and ability to change.
- I cannot change the past, but I can change my attitudes and actions concerning the present and future.
- When I experience emotional discomfort, I will learn to listen to my feelings.
- I will identify the source of the discomfort.
- I will determine what needs to be changed in myself or in my relationships, and I will take steps to relieve that discomfort.
- If necessary, I will change situations or relationships that cause me pain.
- I will not tolerate situations that create turmoil, anxiety, or despair.
- Instead, I will ask God for wisdom and understanding and guidance regarding choices that I have.
- I will not remain locked into any relationship, role, behavior, or attitude that jeopardizes the balance, health, and serenity that God desires in my life and in my relationships.
- Change is necessary for growth, and with God's help, I am capable of making changes in my life.

After the divorce, I started attending an exercise class called New Life Aerobics at the church. The owner choreographed aerobic dance workouts to contemporary Christian music. She was also the fitness director at the corporate office of a large Christian-owned company. I loved exercising while dancing to God's music. It helped me feel better because it was good for my mind, body, and soul. I moved past my bad marriage.

A year or so later and after a lot of hard work, I became a certified aerobics instructor with New Life Aerobics and taught a class. I worked full-time during the day, but twice a week, after work, I taught aerobics. At the end of class, the ladies shared prayer requests, and I prayed with and for them. What a miracle to be able to take the skills I had learned from being a majorette (knowing how to memorize dance routines) and use them for God's glory, to minister to others. God is good!

Chapter 10 - Healing Through Journaling

I continued to seek counseling, and it was recommended that I journal. It's healing to the soul to get feelings and thoughts out of your head and on paper. I encourage you to try it. Journal entries or letters are not to be sent to anyone and should never be posted on social media. I'm thankful social media didn't exist when I was going through my healing process. When my depression hit, the feelings could paralyze me and distort my thinking, and I didn't understand what was happening. Below are a couple of excerpts.

1/23/1991 10:00 p.m.

I can't remember when I've ever felt so lonely. I could do a lot of tasks around the house like cleaning and straightening up, but I can't seem to motivate myself to do anything. Please, God, help me out of this. I should have never gone out with that guy. The last thing I needed was a man to think and worry about. I need to learn to take care of me! It's going to take all the strength

I have to get out of this depression of being unemployed. I can't handle the thought and depression of how I handle relationships. I don't understand what happened that he wouldn't want to call again, but then I never do. You'd think I would have an idea of what my problem is by now. What a charity case I am. Am I ever going to be able to interact with other human beings? I don't think I'll have to worry too much at this point. I may not ever see any again. I feel like I'm at the edge of the earth, alone, never to be found by another living being. Is this how it felt growing up? Is this why I'm so afraid to be alone now, because I think and feel that it will never end, that I have no control over it and life will always be this lonely? What I want now is some fun in my life. I want to teach a couple of aerobics classes, work part-

time, maybe finish school. I have got to get with Linda! This is the way I really want to go. Please, God, help this come about. Her New Life Aerobics ministry is a real ministry. Please let me be part of this. *(God answered this prayer by letting me teach aerobics and eventually get my associate's degree.)*

I know Mom is in much pain, and it hurts me too seeing Michael locked away, but it may be his only chance for help. It is not my responsibility to relieve Mom's pain. I can't. I need to take care of my own pain and hurt from this. Mom has to take care of herself. She should have thought about herself long ago, but she can't feel self-worth unless everyone is in her constant care. I will not allow her to run my life anymore. Please, Lord, O God, in Jesus's name, I beg you to help me get to work so I don't have to ask her for help, please.

God, help me to remember my worth is found in what your word says about me and not how man thinks. Thank you, Jesus.

2/13/1991 2:00 p.m.

What just happened? I'm so depressed. Mom just dropped by again. I have no privacy. I have been violated again. It's supposed to make it all right because she brings me a gift. She brought towels. I'm supposed to be thankful, but instead I feel angry because she doesn't have enough respect for me to call first. Then I feel guilty for being angry. In less than ten minutes, she drops several bombs on me and leaves, hoping I'll take her sadness and frustration. She walks in the door saying she has to leave (literally). Then she says she has another growth they found on her Pap smear that will have to have laser surgery to be removed. She's sad about that, but she has no one to turn to for comfort. No one but me, and I can't comfort her anymore. She tells me how my stepdad is driving her crazy and she doesn't know how much longer they will be together (wish I had a dime for every time I heard that). She's tired of being cussed out by him, and she tells me how he's acting, which happens to be the same things he's always done. You'd think by now she would face it. Neither Mike nor I are living at home to distract her from the reality and pain, nor does she have the alcohol (she stopped drinking & started going to church with me and then by herself). However, if I would just be the codependent daughter that she raised, I could take her pain, be there for her, and fix the family.

My little girl feels frightened (counselors recommend comforting your wounded inner child, which is what this journal entry reveals). She feels like a victim again. I feel panicky. It's OK, darling. I love you, Sharon, I'm here for you. I'm an adult who loves you and will take care of you. Jesus is here with us, and we'll get past this. Your fear is understandable, because no one can take that type of sadness, misery, and craziness and not be affected.

They're [my mom and stepdad] adults; they have to help themselves. I can't and don't need to take care of them. Only they can control their lives, not me. They have made their own choices, and they will have to make the right ones to get out of their circumstances. I am a frightened, isolated little girl who needs their love but won't get it from them. I will take care of what I can control and do something about me and my *life. Jesus in me, we will be all right. Jesus loves the little children. Jesus loves me this I know, for the Bible tells me so. Little ones to Him belong, they are weak, but He is strong. Yes, Jesus loves me!*

I struggled with my healing process and tried to journal my feelings, even when they didn't make sense.

Around 1990, my brother was arrested for attempted child molestation, which was rare and unheard of at that time. Molestation should never be commonplace, but unfortunately it is much more prevalent today than it was in the early '90s. My brother was living in an extended-stay motel, and the cleaning lady often brought her daughter to work. When the mother was busy, my brother lured the little girl into his room and shut the door. When the cleaning lady discovered the girl missing, she used her master key to enter his room, and she testified in court that he had his pants unzipped and open and was sitting on the bed.

Thankfully, the mother found the little girl in time. My brother went to jail, as he should have, but at the trial, he was evaluated by a psychiatrist and found not guilty by reason of insanity.

Here's my journal entry at that time:

My brother is hopeless, according to the doctors. He has an IQ of 70 (that of a 10-year-old), can't function around people to carry on a conversation, and believes the TV is real life. Medication can't help him, and he should be institutionalized. Just so that I can feel some of Mom's pain, she wanted to know if he could stay with me for a while.

I could hardly believe it when I read this journal entry for the first time in over thirty years. I can't believe Mom expected *me* to allow my brother, a mentally ill possible child molester and dangerous person, to live with me. It seemed his needs were always more important than mine, and obviously I was still living in the old house she owned.

After several years of counseling, I realized I needed to remove myself from Mom's control and get out of the old house. When families are dysfunctional and enmeshed, it can be hard to live your own life without resentment or anger from codependent relatives.

I lived in that house for eight years. Mom didn't ask for rent, but she thought she should be able to dictate my life and use me as her emotional garbage dump. She had the money she inherited (after paying cash for a brand-new BMW) but didn't want to help me move out of the house. She said I should stay there and she didn't want to give me money because she had paid for my wedding several years prior, implying I'd wasted her money since the marriage had ended.

The house was located in an area that was becoming increasingly dangerous, so I begged her to sell it and give me part of the money to purchase something on the northwest side of Atlanta. I wanted to live near the church and friends. I finally had friends who I wanted to be close to, and I wanted to move to an area with plenty of good jobs. Cobb County had the best opportunities in the late eighties and early nineties.

A counselor helped me realize I could not expect Mom to do anything for me, and the money she inherited was hers and I had no legal rights to it. I could sit paralyzed and angry about it or I could make my own way, with God's help, and get what I wanted.

However, in December 1990, I couldn't figure out what God was doing when the church downsized and I lost my job. I wanted to stay in full-time ministry, but I went back into the corporate world and realized I could minister to those around me, wherever God placed me. But sadly, I couldn't move out until I got another job.

The experience I received at the church allowed me to apply for a secretarial job at IBM. This would be a huge opportunity to work for a company that paid well and had great benefits. Around the time I applied for the IBM job, I started dating an inappropriate guy. I had a long history of those. He convinced me to visit an old friend. Of course, this "old friend" was smoking marijuana when we arrived at her house. She teased me about not smoking anymore, so I succumbed to peer pressure and took a few draws from a joint. I had been drug-free for over five years but decided one time wouldn't hurt. The next day, I received a call from IBM saying they were interested in possibly hiring me, but I needed to proceed to the next step in the interview process, which would include a drug test.

I couldn't believe I would have to worry about the results of a drug test. If this had happened any time over the past five years, I wouldn't even have thought twice about it. I was terrified. I thought I would miss a great job opportunity because of one mistake. As soon as I hung up the phone from speaking with IBM, dread and fear entered me, and I clearly heard God's spirit speak to me, as if He were standing beside me. He said, "You've been delivered, and there should be no place in your life for these things."

I took the drug test, and for days I worried until finally I received word that I'd passed! God saved me once again, and He gave me the job at IBM. I couldn't believe the sovereignty of God and how desperately He wanted me to follow Him, without reservation. God, the creator of the universe, cared enough about *me* to teach me a valuable lesson about drugs! I am thankful God used that incident to scare me straight and teach me the importance of following Him. I ended that dating relationship and never touched drugs again!

I still had problems with self-esteem, which made it hard to make wise choices when it came to men. I was searching for acceptance in the wrong places and directed my unresolved anger inward with self-destructive behavior. But eventually I was in a Bible study called Father's Heart, where "soul ties" were discussed. I had never heard that term before.

I discovered that when we have sex with somebody, we form soul ties—bonds that can tie us emotionally and spiritually to someone or evil spirits. There are books dedicated to the topic of "how to break spiritual soul ties." God never intended us to tie ourselves to others through sex outside of marriage. There's a connection that happens between partners that should be confined to marriage. Satanic spirits can connect to us in acts of deviance. The connection can also happen through acts of impurity without having sex. It can be through impure thoughts or looking at pornography.

If you have had impure actions, it's important to pray and, if possible, have a pastor anoint you with oil and pray over you that God would break any and all soul ties in your life. I encourage you to research the subject of "breaking soul ties" if you think you need to address those bad spirits in your life.

Breaking these ties allowed me to finally get free from those horrible experiences, and I could start to understand my value. I was able to rebuke those soul ties and remove them from my life! Upon completion of the Father's Heart class, participants went through water Baptism (even if it was a second time), which gave me a fresh, clean start with God, to go forward and sin no more in this area.

1 John 1:9 (KJV) If we confess our sins, he is faithful and just to forgive us our sins, and to cleanse us from all unrighteousness.

I also purchased and listened to a cassette tape series by Marilyn Hickey entitled "How to Break Generational Curses." I listened to the entire series and got down on my knees and asked God to stop the curse of chemical addiction and mental illness in my family. I prayed it would end with me and not affect me or anyone else in my family. You can do the same.

Luke 1:50 (KJV) And his mercy is on them that fear him from generation to generation.

Thank you, Jesus!

After I started working at IBM, I began looking for a place to rent in Cobb County. I found a duplex with two bedrooms, two and a half baths, a fireplace, and a fenced backyard. By now I had a husky dog, so I needed a fence. I loved the duplex and the price. After I moved in, I realized how close it was to where all my friends lived and how close it was to the church. I already knew it was a shorter drive to where I worked in midtown

Atlanta, but happily, not long after I moved to the duplex, my office moved even closer, to Cobb County.

God had directed me to the perfect place to live, one that I could afford...just in time. I say "just in time" because five months after I moved, my stepfather passed away. If I had not left the old house Mom owned before he passed away, I don't think I would have ever moved an hour away from her. I would have felt the need to stay and take care of her. The guilt to stay near Mom would have kept me under her control, but she was only fifty-nine years old and in good health when he died and, I assumed, quite capable of taking care of herself.

Chapter 11 - God's Grace

After eight long years in the old house owned by Mom, I was finally living in my own place. I was working a job that I loved, paying rent, and making my own way. I actually started having fun. I enjoyed life with friends from church, and the relationships I developed helped my healing process. I was working on social skills and how to relate to my peers and others outside my family. Michael Howard, my future husband and the man I met while working at Mount Paran Church, had broken up with his girlfriend. We found ourselves with the same group of friends and getting to know one another. We developed a close friendship, but I always thought he was too old for me since he was twelve and a half years older.

I was, however, diagnosed with clinical depression, which is different than "situational depression." Depression (major depressive disorder or clinical depression) is a common but serious mood disorder. It causes severe symptoms that affect how you feel, think, and handle daily activities, such as sleeping, eating, or working. To be diagnosed with depression, the symptoms must be present for at least two weeks.

Some forms of depression are slightly different, or they may develop under unique circumstances, but this defines what I was dealing with: Persistent depressive disorder (also called dysthymia) is a depressed mood that lasts for at least two years. A person diagnosed with persistent depressive disorder may have episodes of major depression along with periods of less severe symptoms, but symptoms must last for two years to be considered persistent depressive disorder.[5]

Wikipedia defines clinical depression this way: "**Major depressive disorder (MDD)**, also known simply as **depression**, is a mental disorder characterized by at least two weeks of low mood that is present across most situations. It is often accompanied by low self-esteem, loss of interest in normally enjoyable activities, low energy, and pain without a clear cause.[6]

I turned thirty and struggled with depression. The fear of completely losing my mind continued to haunt me. Since my father was able to live outside of a hospital until he was forty-five, I figured mental illness was still a possibility for me. I was single and childless and wondered if I had a future at all. I saw how my father, brother, and my uncle Edward lived a drug-induced, sad existence, and Satan tried hard to make me give up and concede to being a mental vegetable the rest of my life. Part of me wanted to give up and thought it would be easier to admit defeat and stop spending money on counselors or working to overcome it all. Was I destined for failure? I asked my counselor if I was crazy and was assured that the very fact that I was asking meant I was *not* crazy. When I was diagnosed with depression, I was actually relieved, because it meant I could receive treatment and live a somewhat normal life. Even though depression is serious, I was not completely crazy. I also found out I had ADD, attention deficit disorder, which helped me understand my inability to focus or to block out distractions. As doctors began to prescribe medications such as Prozac, Ritalin, and others, I felt as if I was admitting defeat. Shouldn't I just trust God? But the struggle with depression is real, and people need to realize the creation of these medications made it possible for many people to live outside hospitals and to have fulfilled and purposeful lives for God!

When I didn't like the symptoms I felt from taking a certain medication, or if it made me feel numb, I told the doctor and tried something different. When I took Wellbutrin, it seemed to help the symptoms of depression. I learned there are brain chemical imbalances that can be managed with these medications. Depression seems to have a biological component. Research suggests that depression may be linked to changes in the functioning of brain chemicals called neurotransmitters, so this medication helps regulate those chemicals.

I settled on one medication, Wellbutrin, which I still take today. Several times over the years, I've stopped taking it, thinking I was better and could go without medication, but when I was off it for a little while, I would feel stressed and notice the symptoms returning. So now I'm thankful for it and realize it helps. I wish the church (in general) would stop shaming people and making them feel as if they don't have enough faith if they take antidepressants. No one would tell a diabetic to have faith and stop taking their medication. So why do they do that to someone with brain chemical imbalances?

You'll see in my journal entry, the reason I had to find help. It shows just how desperate I could get. I began to see a pattern in my life too. I would accomplish something positive and then sabotage it by letting a man abuse me. I had to find ways to stop this behavior.

2/5/94 Saturday 11:10 p.m.

I wish I had some way to finally destroy myself in a painless manner. I can't survive the pain I'm feeling. I'm so sorry to disappoint all those around me. Please forgive me, Jim, for any and all the trouble I've caused you. I wish so much that we could have talked about it so I could tell you how awful I feel and how selfish I realize I am. The pain of losing you is more than I can bear. You are the most selfless and giving person I've ever known, and I don't (didn't) know how to give back. I don't know how to have a loving, giving relationship but thought I could learn. I was wrong. I need to be in a hospital with the rest of my family, but rather than do that, I'd rather die. I wish I could think of some other way to do that other than using the gun. I'm sorry to whomever found me.

Obviously, I did not take my life that night, and I can't even remember who that man was that I referenced. That's how bad I was about getting involved in inappropriate relationships in my desire to acquire love. I got involved in one bad relationship after another. I didn't know how to love, but God was still working on me. God had to work hard to teach me how much I was loved by him. When you recognize God's love and your value in Christ, you learn to love yourself and have a freedom to truly love others.

I began to ask God for wisdom. The promise of wisdom is one of the greatest promises in the Bible, after the promise of salvation. God, the maker of heaven and earth, agrees to impart to us what we need to be successful in this life while here on earth! To be clear, we will never know God fully and cannot be like God, but what a wonderful promise that He will give us what we need. Listen to what the Bible tells us:

James 1:5 (NASB) But if any of you lacks wisdom, let him ask of God, who gives to all generously and without reproach, and it will be given to him.

Prov. 1:7 (KJV) The fear of the LORD is the beginning of knowledge: but fools despise wisdom and instruction.

James 3:17 (KJV) But the wisdom that is from above is first pure, then peaceable, gentle, and easy to be entreated, full of mercy and good fruits, without partiality, and without hypocrisy.

Prov. 8:11 (KJV) For wisdom is better than rubies; and all the things that may be desired are not to be compared to it.

Prov. 12:15 (NASB) The way of a fool is right in his own eyes, But a wise man is he who listens to counsel.

You can look up more verses regarding wisdom: *Colossians 3:16, 1 Kings 4:30, Proverbs 4:7, 1 Kings 4:34, and Ecclesiastes 7:12.*

God blessed Solomon because he asked for wisdom, over anything else. There's many references to wisdom and how God freely bestows it on those who seek Him. **Scholarly knowledge is a noble pursuit, but it means nothing without godly wisdom.**

Here are positive statements I received from one of my support groups that helped my healing and can help yours as well if you will say them out loud and let them sink in.

- I can find outlets today for my anger.

- I can choose to express my anger appropriately and not hurt myself or others.
- I have used anger to protect myself from other feelings of sadness and fear.
- I have vented my anger by using chemicals, food, or relationships and have abused myself and others by my explosive, destructive behavior.
- I believed that if I ignored my anger or somehow cut myself off from it, that it would just go away.
- But it is because I have cut myself off from my true feelings, or was never allowed to express them appropriately, that I lack the skills to resolve them.
- This is the day that I can cease to let anger run my life.
- I no longer have to unjustly direct and vent my anger, actively or passively, on my partner, my children, my co-workers, or my friends.
- I can take all of my feelings to God, knowing that nothing I feel can separate me from His love for me and that He will never cast me away.
- And I can turn to others for assistance and support in understanding, accepting, and expressing all of my feelings, especially anger, in healthy, appropriate, and productive ways.

God has given us control over our emotions so our emotions do not control us. We do *not* have to live by our emotions, but we can live by the Word of God. I felt as though my emotions were out of control when I began the healing process, and I realized I was extremely angry. The words of God are written in the Bible so we can spend time examining them in order to get to know the person and nature of God. How would you trust a person if you didn't know anything about them or had rarely spent time with them? You wouldn't and shouldn't.

I lived in the rented duplex for two years, and then God gave me the desire to purchase my own home—all by myself. I wanted to invest in property instead of simply renting. Several friends and I took a free first-time home buyers' class. I was a thirty-two-year-old single woman who wanted to believe I could be a homeowner. The idea of obligating myself to a loan of that magnitude terrified me, but I was trying to accept that God's will for me at that time was singleness, and I needed to learn to live without an earthly man. God wanted me to lean on and trust Him.

While I was growing up, Mom didn't encourage me to go to college and have a successful career. She didn't tell me I could be or do anything. No, I was told over and over, "Make yourself look attractive to men and marry one who makes a lot of money and can take care of you, so you won't have to work." This was ingrained in me from an early age. There was a time when a counselor had asked what I would like to do, and I couldn't answer because I'd never thought about it, nor had anyone ever asked me that question.

When I was a young girl, I told Mom I wanted to be a lawyer (after discovering my father went to law school), but I was told there was no money to pay for college. And when I said I wanted to be a psychiatrist, I was told it would take too many years of school. I was usually discouraged from dreaming and received negative feedback from Mom, so I learned not to share any desire or reveal things to her. Nevertheless, God was encouraging me to step out in faith and walk in freedom.

I was scared to purchase a home alone, but I tried to listen to God, step-by-step, day by day. There were a couple of homes I wanted to purchase, but they didn't work out for one reason or another. Eventually I discovered that delay to be God's divine protection because the home I ended up purchasing was perfect for me and my dog. God truly blessed me with a two-bedroom, two-bath home with a fireplace, fenced yard, and one-car garage—and at the right price. It was perfect for me.

The monthly payment was just a little more than what I was paying in rent, but the cost of upkeep was scary. And to obligate myself (I had no help from anyone else) with that much debt and responsibility could discourage many people from even trying, but I believed God was telling me to go forward, and He reassured me in a wonderful way. One Saturday morning during the purchase process, I met the Realtor and inspector at the house I planned to buy. As the inspector was finishing his report, we noticed a dove in the bird feeder outside the kitchen window. I mentioned that I loved doves, as they represent the Holy Spirit and peace.

Matt. 3:16 (KJV) And Jesus, when he was baptized, went up straightway out of the water: and, lo, the heavens were opened unto him, and he saw the Spirit of God descending like a dove, and lighting upon him.

Since both the Realtor and inspector were Christians, they agreed with me about doves, and the inspector said, "It's unusual to see a dove on the feeder because they normally feed on the ground." If the dove had been feeding on the ground, we wouldn't have been having that discussion. When the inspection was complete, I drove directly back to my duplex, and as I pulled up to the concrete parking area in front of my rental unit, there on the ground and in my parking space were two doves!

I had to stop the car before I could park and wait on them to walk or fly away. As I sat for a moment and watched them move out of the way, I felt the Holy Spirit and knew at that moment that God was giving me the assurance and peace I needed that I was doing the right thing. They represented His peace and reassured me that He would see me through the buying process and anything else in life. All I needed to do was trust and rest in Him! Anytime after that when I had concern or felt worry creep in, I thought of those doves and God's personal message. God is always trying to speak to us because He loves us so much. Listen and watch what He can do in your everyday life.

I moved into my beautiful home and could hardly believe it. I was so thankful to God and proud to know what I had accomplished, on my own. The first time I took Mom to the house, she stepped out of the car onto the driveway, looked up at the house, and said these words: "I'd sure hate to know I had to spend $75,000 for this."

I tried not to let those discouraging and derogatory words affect me, but they were ringing in my ears when, less than a month later, I lost my job. Before the first mortgage payment was due, I was unemployed. Devastated, I felt like that redheaded stepchild again. What a complete failure.

The day I lost my executive assistant job (I had left IBM a year prior), I went to a house I hadn't even made the first payment on and had no idea what was going to happen to me or the home. As ecstatically happy as I had been about moving into my very own home, I was now just as low and mortified. I thought, "Mom was right. I'm an idiot and should never have tried to do anything on my own and certainly nothing of this magnitude."

I couldn't believe God would let this happen. Was I destined for the rest of my life to get my hopes up only to have them dashed? I thought for sure I had heard from God about buying the home and this was what I was supposed to do. I collapsed on the bedroom floor, crying, "Why God? What are you doing? How did I miss you again?"

After crying for a while, I began to pray and talk to God and to myself. Something inside started to rise and ask, "Do you believe what you've been learning in God's Word? Are you going to truly trust God? Do you believe God can do what He says He can do? Are you going to walk this thing out? If so, you must get up, dust yourself off, and let God work things out." I didn't realize it at the time, but this would be another huge, character-building trial and a big part of my testimony of what God would do in my life. I asked God for His direction and starting making phone calls to look for a job. I quickly learned of an available position within IBM.

I spoke to a previous manager, and he gave me the contact information which allowed me to go back to work at IBM. I was re-employed quickly and never missed even one mortgage payment. I never borrowed or received money to cover the bills. It was a true miracle! I learned to never let God's blessings become more important than God himself. I also learned to *always* trust God no matter what the circumstances look like and never underestimate what He can do.

1 Cor. 2:9 (KJV) But as it is written, Eye hath not seen, nor ear heard, neither have entered into the heart of man, the things which God hath prepared for them that love him.

Deut. 28:2 (KJV) And all these blessings shall come on thee, and overtake thee, if thou shalt hearken unto the voice of the LORD thy God.

Always give God the glory and do not place the blessings above God. Worship the gift giver, not the gift. Also, expect Satan's attack after a spiritual victory. Realize he's a defeated foe, and with God's help, you can overcome anything Satan throws at you.

My new job at IBM set me up for one of the best jobs of my career and gave me the desire to go back to college. I was a secretary—which is a great job, and there's certainly nothing wrong with being a secretary—but about a year later, God gave me the confidence to apply for an inside sales representative position. This was something I would never have thought I could accomplish. Me selling computers? I wasn't a college graduate like most of the other representatives. I didn't have a family member to help promote me within the company (there was lots of nepotism at IBM). So, who was I to think I could go from secretary to sales representative and obtain such a position?

To even believe I could obtain such a prestigious and high-paying job was more than I normally would have considered. To apply for that job would be a huge leap of faith and something rarely done, since not a lot of secretaries believed they could leave their role and take on one in sales.

But I was learning that I was a daughter of the most-high King and to trust Jesus. Even if I didn't think I was qualified for the position, I believed God could do anything through me if I would allow Him. I was learning that with the Holy Spirit guiding and directing me, I could succeed at anything. He cares about every part of our lives and can work through us every day.

I told myself that the only difference in successful people and me was my confidence level. I just needed to have confidence in what I could achieve with God's help. He tells us that in His Word.

Josh. 1:9 (New International Version) Have I not commanded you? Be strong and courageous. Do not be afraid; do not be discouraged, for the LORD your God will be with you wherever you go.

Luke 1:37 (KJV) For with God nothing shall be impossible.

I can't stress enough how important it is to read the Bible and get the word in your heart and soul. It's not enough to have head knowledge of the word. You must really let it enter your spirit so God can change you and accomplish His will through you. He *will* give you strength to face whatever He sends your way. When I started the new job as an inside sales representative, I was sent to Washington, DC, for two weeks' training. Eventually I took short business trips to San Diego, California; Reno, Nevada; Chicago, Illinois; and Nashville, Tennessee. I saw places I'd never seen before and probably wouldn't have seen without that job. I had IBM stock options, a matching-fund retirement account, great pay, insurance, vacation, and the honor of working in the computer industry for one of the biggest companies in the world.

And in addition, IBM looked really good on a resume and opened doors to future jobs for me. Most employees in my role had a four-year or higher college degree, but I was a community college dropout. If I wanted to advance at all, I needed more education, and with tuition reimbursement available, in my early thirties, I returned to school.

Previous college classes I took transferred, so I didn't have to start over. I went to college after work, at night, and obtained an associate of applied technology degree in business management from Chattahoochee Technical College. I also received an Outstanding Graduate award during graduation ceremonies in 1999! I was in awe and wonder of what our mighty God can accomplish if we step out in faith and get out of His way.

I was attending Trinity Chapel Church of God, located not far from my house, where I served as a greeter. My dear friend and future husband, Michael Howard, purchased a home the same year as me and lived less than two miles away. He, however, traveled thirty miles to Dunwoody Baptist Church and was heavily involved in missions there.

God placed Michael in my life and allowed us to be friends for many years in order to teach me the meaning of true friendship and what a man dedicated to God looked like. God's timing was perfect, because I didn't appreciate Michael's sweet spirit at that time, and I still thought he was too old for me. After all, he was twelve and a half years older. God was still working on both of us. We knew each other for over fifteen years before we finally started dating in 2005.

But in 1998, I turned thirty-five, and the one thing missing was a husband and a baby, and I wanted children desperately. My maternal clock was ticking loudly. Friends were getting married and having babies, and I wanted that more than anything, but what do you do when God doesn't do things the way you want? What to do when you don't see your prayers being answered? That was my new trial.

Chapter 12 - Husband #2: Desire Denied

Sadly, sometimes we take matters into our own hands when God doesn't do what we want. I know I'm not the only one who has made that mistake. We think God is telling us to do something when He's not, or we feel we can "help" God.

Make sure you spend plenty of time alone in prayer to hear clearly and to obtain strength. I attended singles' ministry events at church and met a man only four years older than me. I found him attractive and funny, and we started dating. When he proposed to me on stage at an outdoor concert on the Marietta Square—in front of a large crowd and my friends—I wasn't expecting it. It was only eight months into our relationship, and a proposal conducted in such a public way made me feel as if I had no choice but to say yes. But in my head, I thought I'd get out of it later. When I tried to cancel or postpone the wedding, he somehow smooth-talked me into believing it would work.

I think an abuser is an exceptional manipulator, like Satan, and the way he proposed was part of this man's manipulation. However, I take full responsibility for allowing myself to succumb. Even my mother told me not to marry him just because I wanted a baby, but a woman's desire to have a child will make her do strange things. Not to mention, a lot of positive things were happening, and my pattern was to sabotage myself with an abusive man. Please recognize this if it's your pattern too, and please do not ignore the warning signs. They were all there because he had been divorced three times (I was his fourth wife), and he had spent time in jail. If there are details about a man you are embarrassed to tell people, take a second and even a third look at your motives.

I had a great job and a lovely home, and I threw it away because I wanted my way and my desire. Anything you want more than God in your life is an idol, even if it's a child. So always keep God first in your life.

Exod. 20:3 (KJV) Thou shalt have no other gods before me.

Unfortunately, I married him and immediately wanted to have a baby, but he thought we should wait at least a year. I obeyed and took birth control. At the end of that year, it was obvious we already had marital issues, and clearly he had no intentions of having a child. Agreeing to have one was a lie he told me to get me to marry him.

Feelings of despair washed over me like a tsunami. I was in a miserable, abusive marriage with a selfish, egotistical, raging maniac, and I was in my late thirties with a possible second divorce looming. I thought, "How can I call myself a Christian and not make a marriage work?"

I tried everything to make it work, though. We even sold my cute little home and bought a larger home in Powder Springs. We sought counseling, but when we were given homework, we couldn't complete it due to our arguing. We didn't return. He had major anger issues and flew off the handle at any moment. He verbally and emotionally abused me, just as my stepfather had. I began to gain weight, and the heavier I got, the more he chiseled away at my self-esteem by calling me fat. I felt so helpless and trapped and unattractive, especially when he stopped having sex with me. I wasn't sure if it was because I was overweight and he found me repulsive or because he was afraid I would get pregnant. I soon discovered that just like my first husband, he was having an affair.

I felt like that rejected, redheaded stepchild again. This led to deep depression that affected my work, and I lost my job at IBM. By the grace of God, something rose up in me again.

Don't let tragedy be the only time you strengthen yourself in the Lord. After three and a half years and trying many ways to make the marriage work, I realized I'd made a huge mistake. I prayed about my situation and knew God would not want me to remain in an abusive, adulterous relationship, so I filed for divorce.

I wanted to remain in the house, even though I didn't know how I could afford it. After much back-and-forth with a lawyer, he finally signed a quitclaim deed and moved out of our house and in with his girlfriend and her child. How ironic for someone who didn't want another child. Now what was I going to do?

How could I afford a house payment alone, without my good-paying job at IBM?

Even though I went to work with the largest security alarm company in the world, I had no idea how I was going to afford the home on my own, but I continued to worship and serve God. I spent time with Him in prayer and in the Bible like never before. I was completely broken.

Now, I was twice divorced, childless, and about to turn forty. The reality of it overwhelmed me with grief. The realization that I would never have a child started sinking in. I was alone, and my self-esteem was in the gutter. As a Christian woman, I felt like a complete failure. I started to question if I was being punished for past sins. I also struggled with smoking cigarettes. It was one addiction I had picked up again and could not pray away until 2005.

One Sunday morning after the divorce, I entered church feeling totally defeated. I quietly entered the five-thousand-member church and immediately headed to the balcony to hide. It's easy to hide in a church that size. I didn't want to see or talk to anyone except God.

To my surprise and dismay, an elderly woman I knew came up the steps of the balcony and sat next to me. Her husband was head usher, and she worked in the church office. I had never seen her in the balcony before, but she put her arm around me, and for no apparent reason, she began to tell me she had been married twice before. Both previous husbands had cheated on her, and she had never had her own child.

You can image the waterworks that flowed from my eyes. I was a puddle of water in my seat. I had assumed this couple had been married since high school. After all, they seemed like saints. Hearing her testimony ministered to me like nothing I had heard or felt before, at least not since God had delivered me from drugs and alcohol. I was sorry she had experienced that, but it gave me **hope**. Maybe, just maybe, God could forgive me and give me another chance. Maybe my life wasn't over after two divorces. But the thing that ministered to me the most was that I knew she never sat in the balcony, and it was God who'd sent her to minister to me that morning. God cared enough about *me* to tell me to never doubt His love and forgiveness. I was overcome with awe and amazement.

The fact that God cared enough about me—insignificant little redheaded stepchild, me—to send someone to tell me that my life was not over and that He would be there for me every step of the way was completely humbling followed by joy, peace, and hope. Thank you, Lord!

Shortly after the divorce, I had an opportunity to work from home, something I had been wanting to do for a while, but unfortunately the job was part-time. I felt God wanted me to trust Him again because there didn't seem to be a way for me to pay the mortgage by myself, working only part-time.

But God! Not long after I started working part-time, the job became full-time and paid enough to cover the bills. It often looked as if there would be no way I would have enough money to make it through the month, but I stayed faithful to worship and served God and stayed faithful to the tithe and offering. Even when it didn't make sense to tithe, I did. Just as He promises, He took care of me, and there was always enough. I learned early on that God is my source of all things, and if He asked only for 10 percent, I was getting the better part of that arrangement. God is faithful and good, even if it doesn't look like it to those around you! Trust Him in all things.

Ps. 119:68 (KJV) Thou art good, and doest good; teach me thy statutes.

Josh. 1:9 (KJV) Have not I commanded thee? Be strong and of a good courage; be not afraid, neither be thou dismayed: for the LORD thy God is with thee whithersoever thou goest.

Chapter 13 - Childlessness

The hardest thing I've had to endure is childlessness. It's one of the toughest things a woman can experience, and nothing equips us for it. It's not something you get over; you simply learn to accept it. You learn to forgive God, forgive yourself, and forgive society for not seeming to care about your plight. There's a great need and yearning to produce a child of your own flesh and blood with your genes. It's a natural instinct. When it doesn't happen, the pain is practically too great to bear. And that instinct is not reserved for women only. Men experience the pain of childlessness too.

I spent many hours alone with God, expressing my feelings about not having a child. I shouted and shook my fist at God and then immediately knew it was not His fault. People say don't do this, but I found it therapeutic at the time and believe He is a big God and able to handle my pain and anger. The reality of never having a child was sinking in, and this is the time when many people turn away from God and pout. I won't lie, it crossed my mind, but I decided to continue to go to church every Sunday, serve and volunteer at church, and most of all, worship God. Invariably, someone with a baby would sit in front of me at church, and I would have to sit through the service while watching the mother holding her baby. But I attended church anyway, with my hands raised up high, praising God, often with tears running down my cheeks.

I hated talking to people after church because my eyes would always be red and mascara running since I cried every week. I eventually realized it was the Holy Spirit ministering to me. I was trying to trust God and be thankful for the positive things. There's always something to be thankful for in life. Maybe His direction for my life was not what I thought it should be, but I reminded myself that He's omnipotent and knows better than me.

Doesn't He see the end from the beginning? Can I have *anything* in my life that's more important than God? Once again, I turned to the Word of God and started to feel His soothing love and Holy Spirit as I read and studied the Bible. He ministered to me, and I knew God had proven himself trustworthy in the past. Even if life didn't happen the way I wanted, I decided to follow Him.

I knew there were reasons I didn't have a child, some of which I had contributed to. But God knew the mistakes I would make, even before I was conceived, and He loved me anyway. That's what His Word teaches. He knew He could still make something beautiful of my life. I realized we all have burdens to bear, and childlessness happened to be mine.

Having children brings blessings and suffering too, especially as I saw friends struggle with pain caused by their children, and some were raising grandchildren out of necessity. Not having children brings different blessings and different sufferings, and God gives us the ability to handle whatever He gives or doesn't give us in our life.

He also provides individual abilities and strengths, and when you don't have children, you just have to look harder to find those. I recognize I have special gifts that don't include parenting, but they can still bring meaning and purpose to my life. I choose to look at the blessings He *has* placed in my life and focus on those. I let God bring me up from the depths of hell, some of which I created, and I accept the fact that God loves me and wants what's best for me. Let God heal any and all of your pain today by crying out to Him. Do not give up on God. He hears the cries!

I started volunteering with Happy Tails Pet Assisted Therapy with my dog, Jester. He was the perfect dog for pet therapy. I called him my "angel with fur on" because he was a huge blessing to me at a critical time. This dog loved everybody, and we visited an assisted-living home in Powder Springs for eight years! He was an expression of God's love. We enjoyed visiting elderly patients and sharing the love of God with them. Jester's visits brought smiles and happiness to all. I gained such joy from this ministry. God can make something beautiful from every trial.

Focus on the positive and watch God work. Here are positive statements I had to use in my healing process:
- I am learning to set new limits for myself.

- I see myself as valuable and worthwhile to myself, others, and God.
- I treat myself well, and I set limits for myself that are realistic and appropriate.
- No longer will I seek approval by being and doing what I do not willingly choose to do.
- I will not delay in establishing boundaries for myself and my feelings and needs.
- It is important for me to pay attention to my feelings and to learn to say no when I need to.
- I must also learn to ask for what I need if I expect God or others to be able to meet my needs.
- My responsibility is to be clear about what I do or do not need, what I will and will not tolerate as God's beloved child.
- I have every right to exist, to have my feelings and needs respected and valued, and to take care of myself by setting limits that are right for me and affirm my worth as a human being and God's child.
- I also respect the rights of others to their own feelings and needs and will not impose mine on them or demand that they give up their needs in order to meet mine.
- I will respect them, just as I expect them to respect me.

If you're suffering with hurt, loneliness, depression, or a broken heart, please know God is there for you! You may not feel him, but He *is* with you. Jesus tells us:

John 14:18 (KJV) I will not leave you comfortless: I will come to you.

Ps. 118:6 (KJV) The LORD is on my side; I will not fear: what can man do unto me?

1 John 4:18-19 (KJV) There is no fear in love; but perfect love casteth out fear: because fear hath torment. He that feareth is not made perfect in love. We love him, because he first loved us.

Chapter 14 – Third Time's the Charm: 'Peace' of Paradise

I can hardly believe my life today, especially after reading excerpts from my journals. Here's one from 2005:

Mike has always been noncommittal, but I believe God is working this out. I think God means us to be husband and wife, and Mike's going to realize that VERY SOON! Thank you, God, for what you're doing!

Well, my dear, wonderful husband, Michael Howard, and I will celebrate our ten-year anniversary this year (2018)! That journal entry was three years prior to our wedding. I wish I could insert a video of what our love together has become and how much joy we share. God is so faithful and wonderful. As I write these words and "soak in" God's creation in what I consider the most beautiful setting in the world, our piece (peace) of paradise that is our home, I can hardly comprehend it. I call it a "peace" of paradise because I tend to think it's perfect, and it brings me marvelous peace.

As mentioned, Mike was introduced to me at Mount Paran Church in 1989. He and I became close friends through the years while attending events with mutual friends. He's a wonderful, godly man whom I'm blessed to call my husband. God allowed him to be the one constant in my life for over fifteen years before we started dating in 2005. God knew I needed to witness how a real man behaves and respects a woman.

Since I had terrible trust issues and never knew a man who loved and served Jesus, I was able to see for many years that Mike was a man of true character. He served at church and served others. For twelve years in a row, he went on mission trips with his church. He had a friend who became paraplegic after a car accident, and even though he required help, Mike spent a lot of time with him. Mike was a dedicated, hard worker and strove to improve himself. He moved up the ladder at work to become a plant manager with the Cobb County Water Department, all while caring for his family (mother, father, brothers, sister, nieces, nephew, etc.). He was "the real deal," and over the years, my love and trust for him grew into something more than friendship. It became a love only God can create. We developed a deeper, spiritual bond that can only come through time and getting to truly know one another.

I'm endlessly grateful for where God has brought us! It's a miracle I'm alive. Satan tried to not only stop me but also to destroy and kill me, just as Jesus said.

John 10:10 (NASB) The thief comes only to steal and kill and destroy; I came that they may have life, and have it abundantly.

I thank God for the abundant life we have together. We're both retired and volunteer a lot of our time at our local church.

I can try to thank God often, but there's no way to express the gratitude I have for what God has done. He has truly restored what the locust devoured and restored what the devil stole.

Joel 2:25-26 (ASV) And I will restore to you the years that the locust hath eaten, the canker-worm, and the caterpillar, and the palmer-worm, my great army which I sent among you. And ye shall eat in plenty and be satisfied, and shall praise the name of Jehovah your God, that hath dealt wondrously with you; and my people shall never be put to shame.

Four years after marrying, we purchased a home in Newnan, Georgia. Our piece (peace) of paradise consists of 5.67 acres, something I never thought we could afford, with a ranch house (it's nice not to have stairs to climb as we age). Much of the inside was remodeled and expanded to include an apartment, which was something we wanted for our elderly, widowed mothers. There's a sunroom across the back of the house, which is my favorite room. Originally the back porch, it is now enclosed with floor-to-ceiling windows. I love to open all the windows to feel the breeze, smell the fresh air, and hear birds chirping in the feeder attached to the deck. Dogs are often barking in the distance. The sunroom looks out over the grassy backyard, with woods flanking either side of the grass and no other houses in sight. In the summer, the backyard looks like a golf fairway that continues for about a hundred yards until it reaches the lakeshore and a ten-acre, spring-fed lake.

That hot July day we moved into our new home, we were sweaty and exhausted from lifting boxes and furniture but mustered enough strength to walk our two dogs to the shoreline of our new lakefront property and sit by the shore. The two-person wooden swing was already there when we purchased the home, and it's situated under two shade trees, about ten feet from the water's edge. Leaf-filled branches hang overhead with green grass under our feet. Beautiful tranquilizing waters with tree-lined shores were spread in front of us as we sat there thanking God for His wonderful blessing.

I try not to allow one day to go by that I don't sit in that waterfront swing, as there's nothing more calming for me than to sit by that water. Very soon after that first day, we acquired a canoe and eventually a kayak in order to paddle around the lake. My dog, Ty, goes with me in either boat. There's a natural landscape and an inconceivable peacefulness on that lake. I've pinched myself many times to make sure it's not a dream that this beautiful view exists in *our* backyard.

Very often, a breeze comes off the lake directly into my face. Some days the water is as smooth as glass, and other days when the wind is strong, you can hear the waves lap the shore. The view differs every moment. Sometimes you see heads of turtles popping up and down, and other times you hear the splash and watch the ripples from a fish hitting the top of the water. All summer, if you sit lakeshore at dusk or beyond, frogs are the evening music. Hawks often circle the lake and have been known to rest on top of the cross bar of the swing, looking for their next meal. We've had geese, ducks, and even beavers living in the lake. One day, I spotted a snake in the water just before I exited my kayak. Thankfully, I saw him before he saw me.

Regardless of the conditions, it's always beautiful and peaceful. When I sit by the water and take in the scenery, I clearly see God's magnificent handiwork in all of it—the scenery and my life.

Many years ago, while I was learning relaxation techniques in therapy, the counselor would ask me to close my eyes, take a deep breath, and think about a place that makes me feel at peace and happy. Sometimes an entire support group would practice this technique. The goal was to find, in our mind's eye, a place or scene where we could feel relaxed. Each person would envision something different. Some saw themselves at a sandy beach, while others liked snow-capped mountains, but every time, I envisioned sitting on the dock or next to the water of a beautiful lake. In those sessions, I could almost feel the wind gently blowing on my face. That setting was always my go-to happy place. Sitting at our lake in the swing or in one of our boats is that happy place come true. It's perfect! I can visit my "happy place" in person (not just in my mind) anytime I want (weather permitting)! I'm always looking for ways to combat the symptoms of depression, so the water with its hypnotic virtue washes over my soul and works as a natural antidepressant. Every problem in the world seems to disappear when I'm in that swing. It's what I call my "happy place in God," and I cannot thank Him enough for putting it in my very own backyard.

God renews my strength and my spirit in this magical place. If that's not God giving us the desires of our hearts, I don't know what is. What a great and awesome God we serve!

Ps. 37:4 (KJV) Delight thyself also in the LORD; and he shall give thee the desires of thine heart.

Apparently, though, we're never too old to learn a new lesson from God, because when we decided to purchase this property, we were tested. I was so excited when we first visited the home because I knew it was more than what we could have imagined and exactly what we were looking for. But I didn't want the real estate agent to see my exuberance, and I was afraid to get my hopes up. After all, it cost more than we planned to spend, and we didn't even have our house on the market yet. Surely by the time we sold ours, this one would no longer be available. We certainly could not purchase it without selling the home in Powder Springs. We decided to put our house on the market and said to each other, if it's God's will, it will happen.

That was October 2011, and in January 2012, we received an offer on our house. We didn't know if our perfect property was still available. We weren't sure, but we discovered it was and made an offer. After much back-and-forth, a closing date was scheduled in April. We began packing our things in boxes and taking care of moving details. We were super excited. But two weeks prior to closing, the person buying our home couldn't get his finances in order and withdrew his offer. We had to cancel the contract on our dream property.

I cried as I sat in my home office, signing the cancellation papers, and wondered why God would let us get our hopes up for such a perfect property only to have those hopes dashed. But the memories of God's goodness and faithfulness came back to me. Faith began to rise up, and I told God that I trusted Him and if this was not supposed to be our home, there must be a better one (although I couldn't image a more perfect property). Either that or He was protecting us. I trust you, God, no matter what! Nothing is more important than you, and as long as we have you and each other, that's all that matters. So, we listed our home again and waited. There weren't many showings that spring, and we assumed our perfect house would be snapped up and soon sold to someone else.

Three months seemed like an eternity, but I was trusting God and kept saying that if God wants something for us, no matter what it looks like, He *can* make it happen. After all, He can do anything. Finally, the same buyer returned to make the same offer on our house. He now had his financing together. Shockingly, our dream home was still available, but the owner was not welcoming and wanted more money. It had been three months since our original agreement, and no improvements had been made to the property, but he insisted on more money. I was so frustrated with this homeowner, I thought we should stop trying to force things and look at other houses.

We found a remodeled home with a pool on two acres located just off a busy highway in Sharpsburg. We liked it, so we put an offer on it, but I never felt peace. We were moving because we wanted privacy and quiet country living, and this didn't really offer either. It was in a subdivision.

I woke early one Sunday morning around 4 a.m. and lay in bed praying. I told God if this was not the house we were supposed to buy, then He needed to make it clear and tell Mike so that we could make a joint decision. I could not dictate a decision this big. We needed to decide together and know which house God wanted us to purchase. After I prayed, I drifted back to sleep.

Later, Mike and I woke up to get ready for church. Before any words were spoken, I could see something was wrong by the expression on his face, so I asked him what the problem was. I couldn't have been more surprised when he said he'd had a dream or actually a nightmare. He told me that he dreamed he was standing outside the house we had a contract on and was looking up at the gutters, but he began to sink into the ground. It was as if he were standing in quicksand and sinking. It scared him and made him believe it was a warning. And I began to tell him about my prayer, and we realized that God loves us so much, He was protecting us from buying the wrong house. He was speaking to Mike through a dream. Don't limit God and how He speaks!

I think the other house was a test to see if the lake house was going to be an idol. Once God realized we were willing to let it go, it was okay for us to have the lake house. So, God made it happen. He protected us from making a mistake and directed us to our piece (peace) of paradise. We're thankful to be located in a private, quiet part of the county and not in the middle of all the traffic and growth, where we would have been.

My next test came when we discovered I had skin cancer (basal cell carcinoma) on my nose. Why did it have to be on my face, of all places? We discovered it during the house-purchasing process. The skin cancer required surgical removal, a procedure called Mohs.

During Mohs surgery, thin layers of cancer-containing skin are progressively removed and examined until only cancer-free tissue remains. Turned out, the surgery would happen five days after we moved into our dream home. A scar was inevitable, and more cancer was discovered on the other side of my nose. I was living in my dream home but lying on the couch, recovering with a wound and bandage on my nose. It was not how I wanted to meet new neighbors. I also didn't want to look for a new church while I was wearing a huge bandage on my nose, and I had to wear the bandage for six months. That's a long time for us to not go to church or try to find a new church. Unfortunately, I will wear an actual scar for the rest of my life. Just when you think all your dreams are coming true, life throws a curve ball.

Remember, I was taught that appearance was very important. I thought people judged you on how you look on the outside, and some of my self-esteem was still wrapped up in my looks. But God was teaching me the truth! What matters is what is on the inside!

It took time for me to get over the fact that I was never going to look the same or as good as I did prior to surgery, because I would always be disfigured on my face. And what could be a more conspicuous place than on my nose? I did a lot of talking to God, again. But He cared enough to teach me that my identity is not found in any "thing." It's not found in my looks or a home or family of origin! My identity is found only in the Lord Jesus Christ and what He did for me on the cross! It was confirmed to me that I'm a daughter of the King and am loved by God, and nothing else matters. And I was thankful to be cancer-free!

He was confirming what He had been trying to teach me for years. I'm precious in His sight, and it does not matter what anyone thinks about the way my nose, my hair, my body, my skin, or anything else looks on my outside. Also, I learned not to put confidence in things of this world! I thank God for teaching me this valuable lesson and am reminded every day when I look at my scar that God loves me enough to teach me His truth. I also realized what a wonderfully supportive husband I have. Mike comforted me and made me feel beautiful with his love and acceptance.

Mike and I serve in leadership at church. God brought us to a spirit-filled Assemblies of God church, which is a start-up campus. I serve as guest services coordinator (greeter coordinator), and Mike is usher, parking lot attendant, and the person God used to find the building in which the church resides!

We love and revel in our church family and friends. We also enjoy working together on our property, whether it's cutting grass or planting flowers, trees, or tomatoes. We feed corn to the deer and have one doe that seems like a pet because we've fed her for over five years. She keeps bringing her fawns every year, and I even have video of her nursing them in our backyard! Mostly, though, we like hanging out at the lake. Mike fishes while I paddle around the lake in either the canoe or kayak, or I might simply read a book in the hammock. God has truly blessed.

I urge you to trust God and give Him control of your entire life. Surrender to God. Delight in him, and He will direct your paths and bless you beyond your wildest dreams. When I think about the times I wanted to end my life and believed I had no future, I shudder to think what I would have missed. Thank you, Lord, for rescuing me!

Chapter 16 - Faith

One of the many things God delivered me from was distrust. When I became a Christian, I was told to trust a loving Father and have faith.

Heb. 11:6 (KJV) But without faith it is impossible to please him: for he that cometh to God must believe that he is, and that he is a rewarder of them that diligently seek him.

I'm thankful God was patient with me and proved to me He could be trusted and taught me what a loving Father is. I'm amazed at all the other things God delivered me from too, like bad language and cussing, hate, anger, drugs, alcohol, cigarettes, sexual addiction, worry, negativity, depression, and most of all, He healed and saved me from mental illness. Freedom is phenomenal! We never completely "arrive," but whatever my shortcomings, I know if I go to God with a sincere heart, He will deliver me.

By faith, God allowed me to obtain jobs and positions that in my own ability, I could never have acquired. I don't say this to boast in my abilities but only to boast in the power and wonderment of the Holy Spirit. I not only obtained these positions but I also thrived in them. That is something God wants to do for everyone who will rely solely on Him. In all the companies I worked for, I prayed I was used in some way to minister to those around me. The reality of me being an inside sales representative at IBM, selling services for mainframe computers and power backup units to huge corporations for their databases, is beyond anything I could have imagined. I became vice president of sales at a large courier company in Atlanta, and my most recent position was as advertising sales manager with a local monthly publication. When I wanted nothing more than to work from home, God made that happen too. I started my own administrative services business at one time. It overwhelms me to think of God's goodness. Sometimes, I was terrified of the task I faced, but before I left home, I read scripture from Post-it notes stuck to the bedroom mirror and walls. I would do just as Joyce Meyer quotes, "Do it afraid." And God performed what He promised.

Rom. 4: 21 (KJV) And being fully persuaded that, what he had promised, he was able also to perform.

Col. 3:23 (KJV) And whatsoever ye do, do it heartily, as to the Lord, and not unto men.

Ps. 118:6 (KJV) The LORD is on my side; I will not fear: what can man do unto me?

How does an underdog who came from such humble beginnings without even a bachelor's degree become successful and joyful? Only through God! God can promote you and move the world to get you to where He needs you. Have faith in God and know that He can do anything through you. I've done pretty good for a redheaded stepchild! I'm glad to be in "a happy place with God" mentally, physically, and emotionally! To God be all the glory! Trust and have faith that God can do the same through you.

Start by identifying your wounded places and let God change them to your "happy places." I have learned strategies for combating depression, and perhaps they can help you, as well.

1. Routine sleeping habits to obtain plenty of rest each night.
2. Regular eating schedule and healthy eating.
3. Exercise. Get outside for fresh air!
4. Prayer.
5. Read the Bible *daily*.
6. Rebuke Satan when being attacked.
7. Contact a friend.
8. Talk with a licensed Christian counselor regularly.
9. Make a to-do list and accomplish at least one task.
10. Read Christian self-help books from trusted authors and pastors.
11. Be thankful! Give thanks and praise to God because there's always <u>something</u> in your life you can be thankful for.

Joyce Meyer Ministries has ministered to me over the years as I've watched her on TV. I've viewed and listened to her teaching, read some of her books, and followed her daily devotionals. She teaches that the mind is our biggest battlefield and it's not enough to simply get rid of negative thoughts but that we must replace them with positive ones. In 2006, I found a list of positive statements on her website and typed two pages of them that I printed out and started quoting daily. I would speak them out loud to encourage myself. I still have the copy and turn to it occasionally. I encourage you to replace negative thoughts with positive ones by speaking them aloud. Below is my list. You can use these or create your own.

- I love all people (Matt. 22:39).
- I prosper in everything I put my hands to. I have prosperity in all areas of my life—spiritually, financially, mentally, and socially (Prov. 8:18).
- I have humbled myself, and God has exalted me (Luke 14:11).
- I cast all my care on the Lord for He cares for me (1 Pet. 5:7).
- I am a giver. It is more blessed to give than to receive. I love to give! I have plenty of money to give away all the time (2 Cor. 9:7).
- I don't give the devil a foothold in my life. I resist the devil, and he has to flee from me (James 4:7).
- I don't have a spirit of fear but of power and love and a sound mind (2 Tim. 1:7).

- I am not afraid of the faces of men. I am not afraid of the anger of man (Ps. 118:6).
- I am a new creature in Christ: old things have passed away, behold, all things are new (2 Cor. 5:17).
- I am dead to sin and alive unto righteousness (1 Pet. 2:24).
- I am a doer of the Word. I meditate on the Word all the day long (James 1:22).
- I have been set free. I am free to love, to worship, and to trust with no fear of rejection or of being hurt (Gal. 5:1, John 8:36).
- I have compassion and understanding for all people (Jude 1:2; 1 Pet. 3:8).
- I catch the devil in all of his deceitful lies. I cast them down and choose rather to believe the Word of God (John 14:12).
- God opens my mouth, and no man can shut it. God shuts my mouth, and no man can open it (Job 12:14, Ps. 141:3).
- As a man thinketh in his heart, so is he; therefore, all of my thoughts are positive (Prov. 23:7).
- No weapon formed against me shall prosper, but every tongue that rises against me in judgment, I shall show to be in the wrong (Isa. 54:17).

- I am slow to speak, quick to hear, and slow to anger (James 1:19).
- I am always a positive encouragement. I edify and build up; I never tear down or destroy (1 Thess. 5:11; Rom. 14:19).
- I will call to God most high, who performs on my behalf and rewards me (Ps. 17:6-7).
- I don't speak negative things (Prov. 22:11; Col. 4:6).
- I walk in the spirit all the time (Gal. 5:16 and 25; Ezek. 36:27).
- I am an intercessor (Rom. 12:12; Phil. 4:6).
- I choose life—I am worthy to live! Christ died so I could have life and have it more abundantly (John 10:10).
- I have a husband who loves me like Christ loves the church (Eph. 5:25).
- I love myself as Christ loves me and died for me (Rom. 5:6,8).
- I know God loves me (Deut. 23:5; John 3:16; 1 John 4:10-11; Rom. 5:5).
- I do not fear what man can do to me—God is on my side (Ps. 56:11).
- I am anointed by God and have a successful ministry (Matt. 28:19; 2 Cor. 4:1).

Chapter 17 - Conclusion

God's plan is for us to become more Christlike in our mind, body, and soul. God replaced my heart of stone with a heart of flesh, and the layers and layers of walls built to protect my heart from others has been removed and peeled away, one layer at a time. I'm sensitive to others and their needs, which is something I couldn't have done while trying to protect myself from hurt and pain.

Mom and I reconciled and currently maintain a loving relationship. She rededicated her life to Christ many years ago, stopped drinking, and attends a church in Conyers, where she has volunteered in the office every week for over twenty years.

I speak to Mom on the phone almost every day and visit her regularly. She never remarried and lives alone in the same house I grew up in. My husband and I pick her up and bring her to our house to stay on most holidays. When she broke her foot in 2017, she lived with us for four months. Mom and I are able to hug and tell each other "I love you." I chose to do what God commands in His Word and respect my mother, and it has brought us close.

Exod. 20:12 (NASB) Honor your father and your mother, that your days may be prolonged in the land which the LORD your God gives you.

I'll always be thankful Mom was brave enough to get my brother and me away from our dangerous, mentally ill father and managed to provide for our physical needs. She still takes care of my brother, and even though he's lived several different places over the years, he is currently living in an extended-stay motel in Conyers. Unfortunately, my brother and I have never had a close relationship. He doesn't like to be around me or anyone else, so he doesn't join us on any occasion. He's overweight and suffers from diabetes now, so his health is not good. He does nothing but lie around a motel room. I continue to pray for him.

I'm not famous and haven't reached an award-winning pinnacle that some might think warrants a book, but for me to live a fulfilled life outside the walls of a hospital, survive attacks from the devil, and be used by God is a miracle. You can listen to what I've suggested or not, but in everyone's life a little rain must fall. Matthew 5:45 states that it rains on the just and the unjust. So, I'm saying you'll be glad you're prepared with God's umbrella. My desire is to see all saved and free of emotional or mental suffering—and never another suicide.

Ask God to comfort you and give you a sensitivity to His spirit so you can love yourself in order to love and comfort others!

1 Thess. 4:18 (NASB) *Therefore comfort one another with these words.*

John 13:34 (KJV) A new commandment I give unto you, That ye love one another; as I have loved you, that ye also love one another.

1 John 4:7 (NASB) Beloved, let us love one another, for love is of God; and everyone who loves is born of God, and knows God.

1 John 4:19 (NASB) We love, because He first loved us.

One of my biggest fears is public speaking, but in the early 1990s, I decided to face it head-on and gave a speech on the topic of "environment" at a Christian retreat. I wrote these words:

When preparing for this speech, I asked God, "Why do I have to tell everything? How does all this help? What's the point in my telling every detail?" (This was when I was still terribly ashamed to admit in front of a room full of women that my father was mentally ill and that I was divorced, and today it's no less terrifying to lay my life open in a book.)

God faithfully answered with this: "Tell them, you cannot love, relate to, or help others in your life with a four-foot-thick wall standing between you and the rest of the world. You have to get rid of the protection and be part of your environment in order to influence it."

When you're wrapped up in self-preservation, you cannot reach out to and help others. I was so far removed from others that I could not open up to trust or truly love another, and this is our great commandment: "Love your neighbor as yourself."

I was incapable of accepting all God's love for me at one time since I had so many barriers in my life. But patiently God worked with me. Due to the obedience of dedicated individuals who wanted to show God's love, He expressed His love for me a little at a time. It was a kind word, a friend praying for me, a hug, a gift, or a loving note. All these meant Jesus to me and defined love for me.

Out of all the people who have ever lived or will ever exist, no one is exactly like you. God has made you individually unique, and if we don't express Jesus's love in our individual way to others, no one else will. I've met people over the years with true joy and thought, "I know God promises this for all of His children," but I just didn't see how for me. But I write to tell you today that my heart overflows with joy. I know God has supplied my every need and will continue to. My void has been filled, and I pray that if you still have a void in your life, you'll let God fill it in order for you to minister to others.

People need us, and they want real people. They will not respond to our facades, so take a chance, remove the mask, and stop pretending nothing is wrong. Do not suffer in silence. Look at your life earnestly with God, talk about it with someone you trust, and ask God to heal these areas and help you tear down walls that keep you separated from your environment, the walls that keep you removed from situations that could be won for Christ.

Here's a quote from one of my devotionals years ago:

As missionary David Livingstone said, *"Christ alone can save the world—but Christ cannot save the world alone."*[7] God has so ordained that we are essential to that great undertaking. Breathtaking as it is that the Holy God would allow us to be partners with His Son in bringing the world home to Him. Fearful thought, that there are those who will never come home to God unless you or I invite them.

Rev. 22:17a (KJV) And the Spirit and **the bride** *say, Come. And let him that heareth say, Come.*

We are the bride!

No matter what you've been told or made to feel, you are not the "redheaded, unwanted stepchild." We are all children of the most high God. Made in the image of God, we are special to Him.

Eph. 2:10 (NASB) For we are his workmanship created in Christ Jesus for good works, which God prepared beforehand, that we should walk in them.

And He's just waiting for you to enter into your happy place. Look up the word "happy" in your Bible concordance. There are many scriptures on the subject. Here are just a couple:

Ps. 146:5 (KJV) Happy is he that hath the God of Jacob for his help, whose hope is in the LORD his God.

Prov. 16:20 (KJV) He that handleth a matter wisely shall find good: and whoso trusteth in the LORD, happy is he.

A final note:

I will change your name

You shall no longer be called:

Wounded

Outcast

Lonely

Afraid

or…

Redheaded Stepchild

Your new name shall be:

Confidence

Joyfulness

Overcoming One

Faithful

Friend of God

One who seeks my face

Son or Daughter of the King (aka Prince/Princess)

I'm glad God made me the "redheaded stepchild" because it gave me the opportunity to tell you about the amazing work of Jesus Christ that allows me to rest in my "happy place in God." I choose life! I love myself because God created me in His image, and I recognize every human being has value based on the Word of God. This is the power of the Holy Spirit and if you allow Him to work, He will do the same for you.

Gen. 50:20a (NASB) As for you, you meant evil against me, but God meant it for good.

2 Tim. 1:7 (KJV) For God hath not given us the spirit of fear; but of power, and of love, and of a sound **mind**.

Jer. 29:11 (NASB) 'For I know the plans that I have for you,' declares the Lord, 'plans for welfare and not for calamity to give you a future and a hope.'

May God truly bless you.

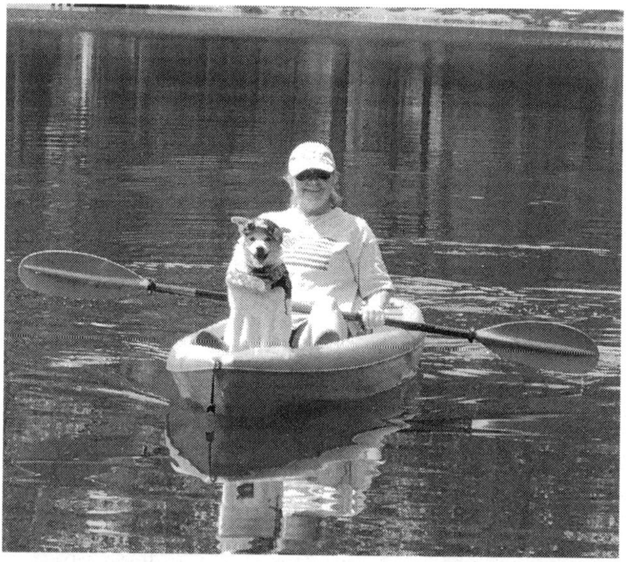

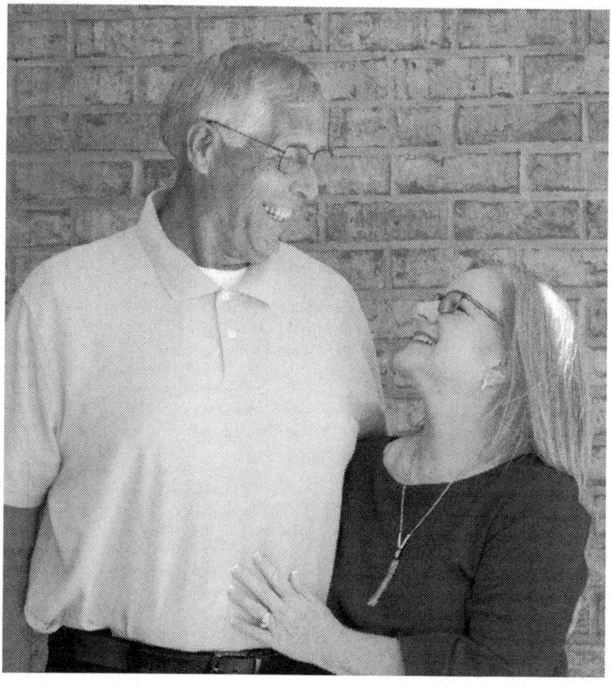

Recommended Reading:

Joyce Meyer—any of her publications

The King's Daughter by Diana Hagee

The Gifts and Ministries of the Holy Spirit by Lester Sumrall

God Calling by Two Listeners

Adult Children of Alcoholics by Janet G. Woititz

Resources:

Griffin First Assembly Church Touch of Healing Counseling Center, Griffin, GA 770-228-2307

https://griffinfirst.org/counseling/

Mount Paran Church of God Pastoral Care and Counseling

2055 Mt. Paran Rd., Atlanta, GA 30327 / 404-923-8700

https://mountparan.com/ministry/culture-of-care/

A New Start Counseling Center (FBC Newnan)

15 W. Washington St., Newnan, GA 30263

770-253-0797 / info@fbcnewnan.org

Mayo Psychological Services, Inc.

1640 Powers Ferry Road, Bldg. 17, Ste. 350, Marietta, GA 30067

770-956-9212 / smayophd@gmail.com

Georgia Crisis Hotline: 800-715-4225

National Suicide Prevention Lifeline: 800-273-8255

[1] http://www.atlantamagazine.com/great-reads/asylum-inside-central-state-hospital-worlds-largest-mental-institution/
[2] http://deepsouthmag.com/2015/10/13/inside-georgias-real-life-lunatic-asylum
[3] https://en.wikipedia.org/wiki/Covert_incest
[4] https://www.goodtherapy.org/blog/emotional-covert-incest-when-parents-make-their-kids-partners-0914165
[5] https://www.nimh.nih.gov/health/topics/depression/index.shtml
[6] https://en.wikipedia.org/wiki/Major_depressive_disorder
[7] https://oneheartint.weebly.com/famous-quotes.html

Made in the USA
Lexington, KY
11 November 2018